Walter Christ, Anne Hueglin, Christian Schmidt, Hildegard Zeilinger
unter Mitarbeit von Ingrid Reinwald und Gerd Sych

English for Bankers

herausgegeben von Walter Christ

2. Auflage

Stam 3401

Stam

Contents

Unit 15 Trade terms and documents

Unit 16 Financing by documentary letter of credit

Kassettenaufnahme
Text im Lehrbuch

Kassettenaufnahme
Text im Lehrerhandbuch

Internet

Sie finden uns im Internet unter: http://www.stam.de

Stam Verlag
Fuggerstraße 7 · 51149 Köln

ISBN 3-8237-**3401**-6

Unit 1
The bank – my working place

About my bank and my job

Part A

Monika Schweiger has just started to work at a German bank. She is an apprentice. Her pen friend Tom Jenkins lives in London. She wants to write to him about her new working place.

Some information about my bank and my job

a Name der Bank	*
b Art der Bank	*
c Rechtsform	*
d Hauptstelle	The * is located in *
e Filialen	The nearest * office is in *
f Zweigstellen	We have about * in *
g Auslandsvertretung	We are (not) * abroad.
Repräsentanz	We have * offices in * and
Zweigstellen	* in the following countries: *
Tochtergesellschaft	We also have * in *
h Eintritt in die Bank	I * the bank * (date)
i Lehrzeit	My * lasts for * years and will be over * (date)
j Arbeitsplatz	Before the first block release course I worked *
k Arbeitsplatzwunsch	After the examination *

1. Please write on a paper all the items missing in the worksheet. Your teacher will help you with the technical expressions.

2. Now write a letter to Tom Jenkins (or your own pen friend) telling him anything you find interesting in your new job including the information from your worksheet.

   If you need some ideas about what to write these questions will help you:
   - How did you find your present job?
   - Which department do you work in?
   - What career opportunities are open to you after your apprenticeship?

The cost of working

Part B

In Tom's answer letter you found enclosed this leaflet informing young people in Britain about the cost of working.

Whether you are about to leave school and hopefully find a job, or you have just done so, that first pay packet or cheque at the end of the month will be awaited with joyful anticipation. Great, you will be thinking. All that money to spend. Unfortunately the reality is that all those £££s are not pocket money; they are what you are going to have to live on.

Firstly – the deductions

Whatever your pay or salary, the figure you will be given will be the 'gross' total. That is, without the basic deductions that all employees have to lose – tax, superannuation etc. (. . .) You will lose up to a third of that gross figure; what you have left is called the 'net'. This is what you have to spend.

Then there's rent

If you are lucky you will be still living at home when you start work. 'Lucky', because if you have to find accommodation on the private market, you can be assured that a large slice of your wages will disappear – just like that!

Most parents, if they can afford to be generous, are happy to be lax about taking cash off you for your 'keep' (rent, food and all those things you take for granted – telephone, heating, toilet rolls, toothpaste etc.) for the first few weeks, months even, until you find your economic feet.

Travelling to work

If you are lucky your job will be close enough to where you live to walk there and back every day (and get some regular exercise into the bargain). But such good fortune is rare. The second cheapest way to travel is by bike. Motorbikes and cars need petrol and involve all sorts of hidden costs like maintenance (expensive), MOT certificates and road licences (legal) and so on. The only guideline is that the further away you work from where you live, the more expensive travelling will be. If you have a relative or neighbour who travels by car there may be the possibility of sharing costs and getting a lift.

Buses are cheap and there are usually discounts to be obtained on a weekly, monthly, even annual basis. Investigate these. If you live in London, Liverpool, Glasgow or Newcastle there is the underground for which you can get season tickets; the same with British Rail if you have to commute to your place of work.

Clothing

Another basic cost that cannot be escaped is the need for proper clothing.

Employers may insist that you dress in a particular way. Some employers may provide the clothing free, while others will expect you to pay for it.

Wherever you work you will have to look reasonably smart, and clothes will have to be kept in good repair and clean. This too costs money.

Food

Fact of life: you have to eat. Maximise on living at home and have a good breakfast and then eat at home in the early evening. Do this and you can get away with a sandwich in the middle of the day. Remember that snacks, consumed to combat boredom as much as anything else, will soon gnaw a hole in your budget if you are not careful.

A packed lunch is always cheaper than eating out. Otherwise your place of work may have a canteen. As likely as not this will be subsidised, so if you're living on your own, it will be cheaper to make this the place for your main meal of the day. (Better for your digestion, too.)

Don't live on 'Fast Food'. You'll always be healthier with old fashioned bread and cheese and an apple than a diet of chips, chips and chips.

Equipment

Will you have to supply yourself with any materials and equipment? Or tools for a specialised trade like plumbing or carpentry? These could well be costs you may not have thought of. If there is anything really major, your Bank may be able to help with a loan or overdraft.

(Midland Bank)

1. Make sure that you have understood the text by answering these questions on the text:
   a What is deducted from the gross salary and how much is left to spend?
   b Why can it be an advantage to continue to live at home after starting work?
   c Rank the different ways to travel to work according to the cost involved.
   d Why is proper clothing so important in some professions?
   e What is the cheapest and healthiest way of eating at work?

2. Write another letter to Tom in which you critically refer to the advice given in the leaflet. Do you agree with the message of the leaflet? What expenses do you have in connection with your job?

Central banks in England and Germany

Monika (M.) is on a visit to her friend Tom (T.) in London. This is part of a talk they had about the central banks in both countries.

T: Do you know that the Bank of England has a nickname?

M: No, I don't. What is it?

T: The Bank is called 'The Old Lady of Threadneedle Street'!

M: Oh, is that so ... it really is quite old, isn't it?

T: Yes, it was founded in 1694, to finance the war of the Grand Alliance against France, and in 1946 it was nationalized.

M: Well, compared with 'The Old Lady' the German Central Bank is a young girl ...

T: When was it established?

M: In 1957 ... but what I'm really interested in is to learn something about 'The Old Lady's' functions.

T: Let me see. Above all it's the central bank of the United Kingdom and as such it is responsible for the note issue ...

M: ... just as the German Central Bank.

T: Right ... furthermore the Bank acts as banker for the government and other banks and advises the British government on economic and financial matters.

M: That's interesting, because the Central Bank is independent and only supports the economic policy of the German government.

T: ... only supports your government?

M: Yes, it doesn't take any orders from the Federal Government.

T: Oh, is that so? That really is different then.

M: Yes, I suppose it is.

T: The Bank acts as financial agent for the government.

M: You mean it carries out the government's monetary policy?

T: Yes, it does and we don't know about the effect that will have.

M: No, I'm sure you don't. But listen ... I'll tell you of another difference between the Bank and the German Central Bank.

T: Another difference?

M: Yes, the German Central Bank has its registered office in Frankfurt ...

T: Of course I know that ...

M: But do you also know that it has nine main branches in Germany?

T: That's new to me. The Bank of England also has eight branches in big towns in Great Britain, as well as its head office in London.

● Summarize the information given about the two central banks in a text of not more than about 100 words.

Part D

Comparison of German and British banks

During her stay in Britain Monika learnt a lot about the British banking system. Back in Germany she finds some useful information about British banks in her notebook.

London and Scottish clearing banks

These are the main high street banks. They are called 'clearing banks' because of their major role in providing chequebook and other payments services. The term 'clearing' is used to describe the system of exchange and settlement of cheques paid into the banks.

There are six London clearing banks operating in England and Wales – Barclays, Lloyds, Midland, National Westminster (and its subsidiary Coutts) and Williams & Glyn's – and three Scottish clearing banks – Bank of Scotland, Clydesdale and Royal Bank of Scotland.

Trustee Savings Banks (TSB)

They have about 1,650 branches and serve mainly the private sector. Traditionally they were organised as a number of separate regional banks, but in 1983 they were merged into one bank for England and Wales, one for Scotland, one for Northern Ireland and one for the Channel Islands.

National Girobank

The National Girobank is part of the Post Office Corporation. It does not have a branch network of its own but provides its services at post office counters. Traditionally the National Girobank specialised in providing payments and related services, but now it offers various other facilities as well.

Merchant Banks

They deal mainly with the corporate sector and their most important activities include the provision of credit to companies, financial advice and investment management. They also help companies to raise more money by advising and organising issues of new shares.

Building societies

The first building society is said to have been founded in Birmingham in 1775. The early societies were set up to help small groups of people save money to buy land and build houses on it.

The building societies are today the banks' greatest high street competitor for private customers. They provide a wider range of financial services and are becoming more and more like the banks.

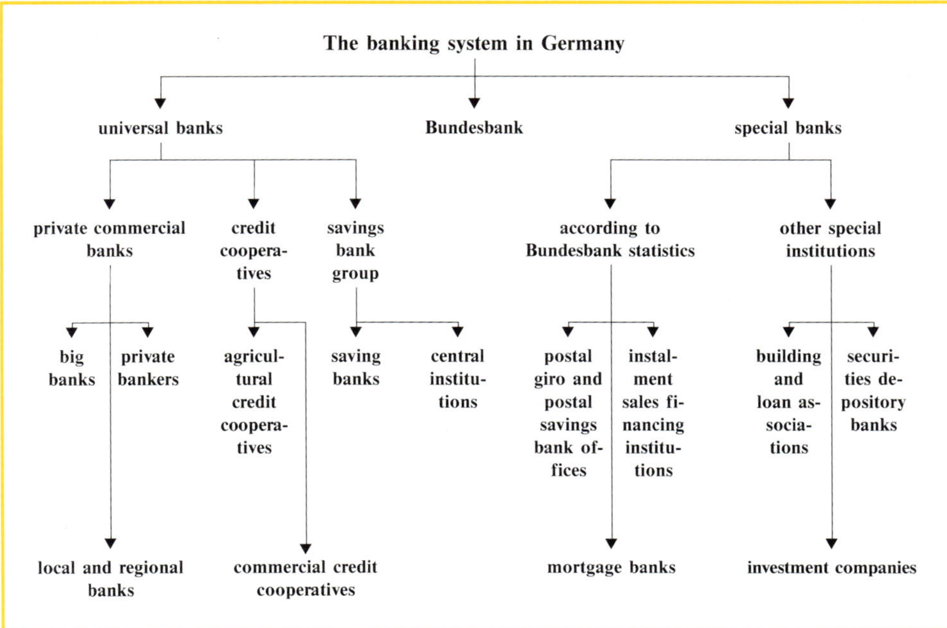

Special banks are all the other institutions that only operate in a limited range of banking business. A classification of these institutions is given in the reports of the Bundesbank. The latter publishes the data of the following special banks in its monthly reports:

- mortgage banks,
- instalment sales financing institutions,
- financial institutions with special functions,
- postal giro and postal savings bank office.

Tom Jenkins wants to know more about the German banking system. Monika can help him by answering these questions in her next letter:

1. What is the German equivalent of clearing banks?
2. Which are the most important German banks?
3. How are TSB organised in Germany?
4. What services are offered by the German "post office savings banks"?
5. Is there anything similar to the merchant banks in Germany?
6. Why are the German 'Bausparkassen' not comparable with the British building societies?

Unit 2
Opening an account

Part A

What do you know about bank accounts?

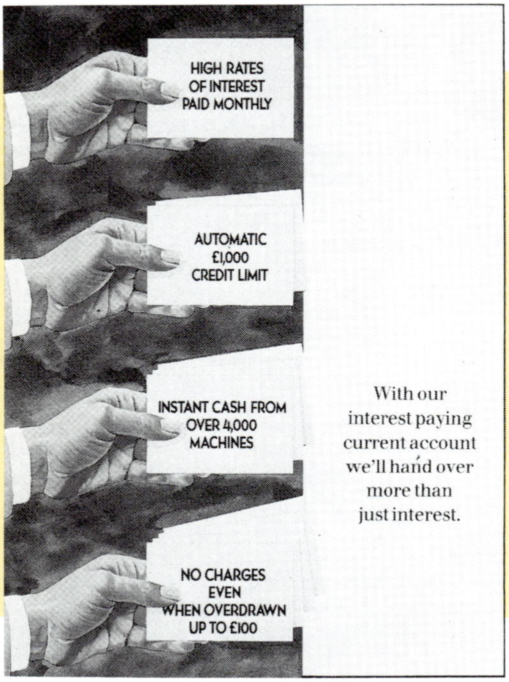

(Royal Bank of Scotland)

Look at the advertisement for an interest paying current account. Would that be an ideal account for you?

Which statements about each type of bank account are correct?

1 The Current Account:

- **a** Money is constantly paid into and withdrawn from a C.A.
- **b** The balance of the money in the account, therefore, frequently changes.
- **c** With a current account you can earn a lot of interest.

2 The Savings Account:

- **a** You can overdraw the account whenever you want.
- **b** The savings account is intended for the accumulation and investment of capital.
- **c** All deposits and withdrawals are entered in the savings book, where the current balance is shown.

3 The Time Deposit Account:

- **a** It is used for the short to medium term investment of larger amounts (not lower than DM 5 000.00).
- **b** No interest is earned on Time Deposit Accounts.
- **c** It is used for standing orders.

Opening an account

Jane Bolder (J. B.) went to Germany to work there as a secretary at a language school. One of the things she had to do first was to open a bank account.
She went to the branch of a bank not far away from her flat. Gerd Heller (G. H.), a young bank clerk, was at the counter.

G. H. Good morning. Can I do anything for you?

J. B. Yes, I want to open an account and I'd like to have my salary paid directly into it.

G. H. Oh, I see. I think a current account would be right for you.

J. B. How much interest do I get for my money with that account?

G. H. For a positive balance you get half a per cent. That's not much but you should consider that we offer a lot of extra services in connection with a current account. It's not only that your employer may transfer your salary to the account. You can also pay in money, withdraw money and transfer money from your account to other accounts.

J. B. You mentioned a positive balance. Does that mean that I can't get a credit with this account?

G. H. No, you can overdraw your account up to a fixed limit. This limit or overdraft depends on your regular salary. We can grant you an overdraft facility being three times more than the amount of your regular salary.

J. B. Well, I would also like to have cheques and to use that account for regular payments.

G. H. That's no problem. You can have as many cheques as you like and we offer standing orders for regular payments such as rent, hire purchase, insurance premiums etc. For payments with variable amounts like telephone bills our direct debit system can be used.

J. B. That sounds quite good. Well, I saw a cash dispenser at the entrance of this branch. How can I use it?

G. H. As a current account holder you get Eurocheques and a Eurocheque card which you can also use for the cash dispenser. There is a small additional fee for this service.

J. B. An additional fee? What are the basic costs for a current account?

G. H. That depends on the number of bookings on your account. But you should know that five bookings each month are free. Furthermore you have to pay for the bank statements. We can send you the statements biweekly or monthly. If you come to this branch to collect them you won't have to pay postage.

J. B. Well, it would be much better if there were no costs and if you could offer a higher rate of interest but I need such an account. So what must I do to open a current account?

G. H. You will see that our bank's service in connection with your current account is very favourable for you. Please wait a moment. I have to get an application form ...

1 True or false? Give reasons for your opinion.

a A current account is used for savings.
b If an arrangement is made with the bank, the account may be overdrawn.
c Many banks debit a basic charge per month regardless of the number of transactions.
d If you pay with a cheque, you pay in cash.

2 Complete these sentences. Write the answers on your own sheet of paper.

a I have an account ___ the Midland Bank.
b She has only DM 60.00 ___ her account.
c What does the abbreviation C. A. stand ___ ?
d What is the number ___ the branch of Lloyds Bank?
e He paid ___ cash.
f Who made ___ the cheque?
g Please fill ___ the form.
h I'd like to pay ___ cheque.

3 What are the advantages and disadvantages of a current account for the customer?

Advantages	*Disadvantages*
– You can pay in money.	– If you overdraw the account, you will have to pay interest.
– ___	– ___

Complete the list on your own sheet of paper.

4 Find the noun. Find a context sentence for each noun or verb.

a to withdraw	**c** to remit	**e** to apply
b to overdraw	**d** to arrange	**f** to sign

5 Find the missing word.

a If you are in the red, your account is ___.
b ___ is what you pay for borrowing money.
c The document the bank sends you showing all your transactions is the ___
d You've taken more money out of your account than you had in it. So you have an ___.

Part C Documents: Statement of account, application form

For each new customer, the bank fills in a form which gives the bank some background information, e. g.

– full name and address of the customer,
– his/her occupation and the employer's name and address,
– references which will be asked for (in England).

Most important, a specimen signature is given. This is the "photograph" by which the bank will recognize its account holder and carry out account holder's orders. Any signature on an order to the bank (for example a cheque) must always be the same as this specimen.

1 Document: Application Form for Opening Accounts and Securities Deposits

An **COMMERZBANK**
AKTIENGESELLSCHAFT

Kunden-Nummer — Wird von der Bank ausgefüllt —	
Kontenbezeichnung:	

Datum: ____________________

Antrag auf Eröffnung von Konten und Depots

Ich bitte Sie, für mich Konten und Depots zu führen.

Persönliche Angaben	
Vorname	
Zuname (auch Geburtsname)	
Straße, Haus-Nr.	
PLZ, Wohnort	
Beruf	
Geschäftszweig	☐ selbständig
Staatsangehörigkeit	
Geburtsdatum	
Geburtsort	
Telefon-Nummer	

Ich erbitte Kontoauszüge ☐ täglich ☐ wöchentlich ☐ monatlich

SPECIMEN

An English speaking person wants to open an account with your bank. You are the bank clerk. Ask for the necessary details in order to make out the application form above.

This is an oral exercise. Do not fill in the form.

2 Look at Markus Lambert's statement of account and make questions about the following details.

a Markus Lambert's account number
b The date of the statement
c The old balance
d The new balance
e The transfer of 25 March
f The payment of DM 50.00
g The number of entries on the debit side of the account
h The kind of payment on the credit side of the account

Prima-Nota-Nr.	Wert	Text, Verwendungszweck	Scheck-End-Nr.	Umsatz Umsatz Soll = S Haben = H
	25.3	Überweisung		103,50 S
	30.3	Gehalt		480,00 H
	30.3	Dauerauftrag		50,00 S
	30.3	Rundfunkgeb.		19,80 S
	30.3	Scheck 333789		299,00 S
	05.4	Scheck 5654482		150,00 S

Geben Sie bitte auf Überweisungen, Aufträgen und im Schriftverkehr Ihre Kontonummer an.

Stadtsparkasse Neuss **Konto-Auszug**

SPECIMEN

Herrn/Frau/Fräulein/Firma

Herrr
Markus Lambert
Kirchweg 18

41468 Neuss

Auszug	Summe Soll-Umsatz		Summe Haben-Umsatz
7	622,30		480,00
Blatt	**Sollzinszahlen**	**Überz.-Zinszahlen**	**Habenzinszahlen**
1		4,27	
Anlagen	**Letzter Auszug**	**Valutensaldo**	**Buchungstag**
1	20		05.04.
Alter Saldo (Soll=S/Haben=H)		**Neuer Saldo (Soll=S/Haben=H)**	
H 350,75		H 212,72	
Schecks und Wechsel schreiben wir Eingang vorbehalten gut.		**Konto-Nr.** 142 016 978	

Fernruf: Sa.-Nr. 02101 · 2051 Beanstandungen richten Sie bitte unter Angabe der Primanota-Nr. an unsere Revisionsabteilung Ruf * 205424. Irrtum vorbehalten!

Part D — Dialogue: Joint account

- To continue the conversation (Part B) translate the following part of a dialogue into English.

G. H. Sind Sie verheiratet?

J. B. Ja, ich bin verheiratet, aber mein Mann ist noch in England. Ich suche gerade nach einer größeren Wohnung, so daß er nachkommen kann.

G. H. Möchten Sie jemandem eine Handlungsvollmacht erteilen?

J. B. Nun, ich möchte, daß mein Mann von meinem Konto Geld abheben kann, wenn er nach Deutschland kommt.

G. H. In diesem Fall brauchen wir die Unterschrift Ihres Mannes. Bitten Sie ihn doch, bei uns vorbeizukommen.

J. B. Er wird in etwa zwei Wochen kommen. Reicht das?

G. H. Ja, natürlich. Würden Sie bitte das Antragsformular unterzeichnen und eine Musterunterschrift auf dieser Karte leisten?

(Sie unterschreibt.)

G. H. Vielen Dank. Wieviel möchten Sie einzahlen? Der Mindestbetrag ist 1,00 DM.

J. B. Kann ich 10,00 DM einzahlen?

G. H. Ja, selbstverständlich. Hier haben Sie Ihre Kontonummer. Ich fülle den Einzahlungsschein für Sie aus.

J. B. Vielen Dank.

Part E — Listening: Opening a current account

1. Why does Thomas Sterling need an account?
2. What can a bank customer use his C.A. for?
3. Why does Ingrid Pohl ask for Thomas Sterling's passport?

Unit 3
Types of accounts

Different types of accounts

Part A

1 Can you explain these different types of accounts? There are some example sentences below which can possibly help you.

- current account
- savings account
- time deposit account
- safe custody account
- deposit account
- joint account Gemeinschaftskonto
- loan account
- cheque account

Example sentences

a A current account or a cheque account is probably the most convenient solution for an employee as it is easy to withdraw money and make transfers.

b If you have some money to spare then you could open a deposit account or savings account.

c You can leave your valuables like jewelry or insurance policies in safe custody with a bank.

d Joint accounts are usually opened by husband and wife, although it is not uncommon for other people to open such accounts.

e If you need a major item – perhaps a car or a stereo – your bank might grant you a personal loan and you would repay a fixed amount each month for perhaps two or three years.

2 And what is special with the share account?

(Abbey National Building Society)

MEMBERSHIP

As a holder of a Share Account, you are a member of the Society and are bound by its Rules. A copy of the Rules is available at any branch.
Abbey National maintains adequate, readily available funds to meet withdrawals. The Society, however, reserves certain rights relating to withdrawals, as set out in the Rules.

INTEREST

Interest is calculated daily on every single pound and credited to your account after close of business on 30th June and 31st December. Your money starts earning interest the day after we receive your investment.

INCOME TAX

You will not have to pay basic rate income tax on your interest as we will discharge that liability. You must, however, include the actual interest received in any return of total income you make to the Inland Revenue.
We account to them in respect of basic rate income tax on all investment accounts. If you pay tax at a higher rate, it will be assessed on the actual interest paid, grossed up the basic rate. You cannot reclaim tax already paid by Abbey National.
The Society is required each year to supply to the Inland Revenue particulars of certain interest paid or credited to investors.

Bank accounts in Germany

Daniel Heath (D. H.), an English student, enters the branch office of a local bank in Germany. Christine Müller (C. M.) is behind the counter.

D. H. Good morning.

C. M. Good morning, sir. Can I help you?

D. H. I'd like to open an account, but I need some information about the different types of accounts here in Germany.

C. M. O.K. Here is a booklet – written in English – which tells you everything about our bank and the services we offer.

D. H. That's very kind. But I think that's not so much what I really have to know. Perhaps you can help me now to find the right type of account.

C. M. Certainly. Well, if you want to make your payments by cheque or transfers you need a current account. You can also make use of standing orders or direct debits on the account to pay your monthly bills.

D. H. That's really what I need. But what about interest if I don't spend my salary in the first weeks?

C. M. With a current account you don't get much interest. It's only half a per cent on your balance at present. But it is possible to transfer the money you don't need for payments to a savings account.

D. H. Is that the same as a deposit account?

C. M. Yes, it's just another name. But let me explain the two types of savings accounts we offer: you may choose either a savings account with a legal or with an agreed period of notice. The interest rate depends on the length of the period of notice – the longer the period the higher the rate of interest.

D. H. And when do I get interest?

C. M. At the end of the calendar year.

D. H. But there may be times when I need money from my savings account.

C. M. If you wish to withdraw some money, you must bring your savings book to the bank. All deposits and withdrawals are entered and the current balance is shown.

D. H. Can I get money at any time?

C. M. No, not in Germany. For accounts with legal period of notice you must give advance notice if you want to withdraw larger amounts. You may, however, withdraw up to DM 3.000 each month without giving notice.

D. H. But if I need the money earlier?

C. M. You may get the money, but then advance interest will be charged.

D. H. Oh, I see. That differs a lot from my bank in Britain.
But another point: can I make transfers to other accounts or draw cheques on this type of account?

C. M. I'm sorry, but that is only possible with a current account.

D. H. Oh, yes. I understand. You've given me lots of information on the different types of accounts, and I'll have to think over whether I'll open a deposit account or a current account.

C. M. Yes, of course, think it over and let us know your decision.

D. H. Thank you very much, you've been very helpful.

Answer the following questions on the text.

a What are the different types of accounts mentioned in the dialogue?
b Which expression is also used for 'current account'?
c What transactions can be carried out with a current account?
d When do customers get their interest paid?
e What does the expression 'agreed period of notice' mean?
f What types of savings accounts do we have here in Germany?
g Are customers allowed to draw cheques on a savings or deposit account?
h Is paying in cash the only way to put money into an account?
i Can customers get money from their savings account at any time?

Part C

Dialogue: Savings account and current account

Say it in English. Form questions and statements.

a Sie fragen einen Kunden am Schalter, ob er schon bedient wird bzw. ob Sie ihm helfen können.
b Sie wollen jemandem die Vorzüge eines Sparkontos erläutern.
c Sie bitten den Kunden, den beiliegenden Antrag auszufüllen und zu unterschreiben.
d Sie geben dem Kunden einen Prospekt zur Information mit.
e Sie werden gefragt, wie hoch der Zinssatz gegenwärtig ist und wie er berechnet wird.
f Sie bitten einen Kunden, zum nächsten Schalter zu gehen, da Sie bereits einen Kunden bedienen.
g Sie fragen Herrn Nomann, ob seine Kontoauszüge täglich, wöchentlich oder monatlich zugesandt werden sollen.
h Ein Kunde will wissen, ob Mindesteinlagen für Anlagekonten mit hoher Verzinsung verlangt werden.
i Sie erklären, daß für die Führung von Girokonten bzw. Gehaltskonten keine Bankgebühren verlangt werden.

Part D

Questionnaire: Comparison of accounts

● Complete the table writing the answers on your own sheet of paper.

	a Current Account	b Savings Account	c Time Deposit Account	d Loan Account	e Safe Custody Account	f Joint Account
1 What are the reasons for opening this type of account?						
2 What is the interest rate on this type of account?						
3 Can you draw on cheques or make transfers?						
4 How much does your bank charge for maintaining this account?						
5 Is it also possible for other people to withdraw money?						
6 How does a customer know how much is in the account?						

Part E

Listening

Text One: Types of account

Text Two: The „ins“ and „outs“ of an account

Text Three: Selling coins and bullion

Text Four: Keeping valuables safe

Unit 4
Money transfers

How the German money transfer system works

Part A

To transfer a certain sum of money from one account to another, the customer has to complete a three-part form which he gets from his bank.

The following details have to be filled in:

1 name and address of the beneficiary,
2 the code number of the beneficiary's bank,
3 the account number of the beneficiary,
4 a reference to the purpose of the payment,
5 the amount of money to be transferred,
6 the customer's account number,
7 the customer's name and address,
8 the date and the customer's signature.

Here you see a specimen form for a transfer order:

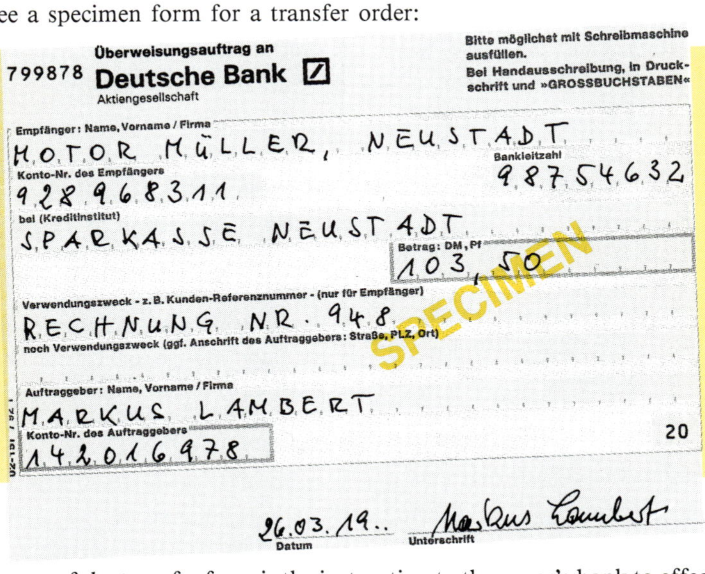
Überweisungsauftrag an
799878 Deutsche Bank
Aktiengesellschaft

Bitte möglichst mit Schreibmaschine ausfüllen.
Bei Handausschreibung, in Druckschrift und »GROSSBUCHSTABEN«

Empfänger: Name, Vorname / Firma
MOTOR MÜLLER, NEUSTADT

Konto-Nr. des Empfängers
928968311

Bankleitzahl
98754632

bei (Kreditinstitut)
SPARKASSE NEUSTADT

Betrag: DM, Pf
103,50

Verwendungszweck - z. B. Kunden-Referenznummer - (nur für Empfänger)
RECHNUNG NR. 948

noch Verwendungszweck (ggf. Anschrift des Auftraggebers: Straße, PLZ, Ort)

Auftraggeber: Name, Vorname / Firma
MARKUS LAMBERT

Konto-Nr. des Auftraggebers
142016978

20

26.03.19..
Datum

Markus Lambert
Unterschrift

SPECIMEN

- The first part of the transfer form is the instruction to the payer's bank to effect the transfer and serves as a debit voucher.
- The second part is the copy to be retained by the customer.
- The third part (printed in red) is designed for the beneficiary. It represents the credit to his account.

The payer's bank examines the remittance and passes the credit form on to the beneficiary's bank. The payee is credited by his bank on receipt of the credit form and receives the voucher together with his next statement.

Some ways of transferring money

1. Withdrawals from a current account

Standing orders
A standing order is used when a current account holder authorizes the bank to make regular payments of a fixed amount from the current account e.g. monthly mortgage payments to building societies. When the amount has to be altered, the current account holder has to inform the bank of the new amount.

Direct debits
A direct debit is used either when payments are made at irregular intervals and/or when the amount varies, e.g. a subscription to a club which is increased every year. With a direct debit the current account holder authorizes the bank to make any payment requested by a payee. It is, therefore, the responsibility of the payee to tell the bank of any changes in the amount to be paid and a new direct debit authorization does not have to be signed by the current account holder.

Cheques and cheque guarantee cards
Another form of withdrawal or payment from a current account is by means of cheques. Such payments are often supported by cheque guarantee cards (e.g. Eurocheques) which are issued to some holders of bank current accounts (see unit 6).

Cash dispensing machines (cash dispensers)
Cash dispensing machines are placed inside or outside banks and allow current account holders to withdraw cash without presenting a cheque. The holder is issued a cash card which is inserted into the dispensing machine. The holder then types in his own personal identification number (PIN) and the amount needed in cash. Some cash dispensers have additional keys which allow the current account holder to:

- receive details of the present balance in the current account,
- order a bank statement.

2. Payments into a current account

Paying-in slips/deposit slips
A current account holder can deposit cash and cheques directly with his own bank branch by completing a paying-in slip. A receipted counterfoil is retained by the customer as evidence of in-payment or deposit.

Credit transfers or remittances
The bank giro system can also be used to transfer funds into the current accounts of others. For example:

- Electricity and gas companies receive payments when customers pay bills by completing the special bank transfer forms found at the foot of electricity and gas bills. The form, together with the payment, is handed in at a bank which then transfers the payment to the company's current account.
- Many employees receive their salaries each month through direct transfer into their current accounts. A firm provides its bank with a list of employees, their bank account numbers and the amounts to be paid. The firm's bank then transfers the various amounts to the employees' bank accounts. The firm provides the bank with a single cheque to cover the total wage bill. This use of bank giro is an example of multiple credits because payment is being made into a number of accounts.

Most of the methods of payment into current accounts considered in this part of the unit are also forms of payment from current accounts, for one person's payment must be another person's receipt.

(Adapted from: Lett's Study Aids, Revise Commerce, London)

1. Which statements about the standing order system are correct? Give reasons for your opinion.

   a The bank transfers your payments on certain dates, and you can be sure that they'll arrive punctually.
   b The standing order system is suitable if the amounts vary every month.
   c The standing order is for regularly recurring payments with relatively fixed amounts.
   d The standing order can be altered by the debtor.
   e It is an automated non-cash payment.

2. Which statements about the direct debit system are not true? Give reasons for your opinion.

   a It can be used for both varying and fixed amounts.
   b With direct debiting the payee makes arrangements with the payers so that he is permitted to debit their accounts on a certain date.
   c The debtor authorizes his bank to transfer money at certain dates and intervals.
   d The amount can be altered by the creditor.
   e The account holder has to remember to make the payments.
   f Individual cheques or transfer orders do not have to be written.

3. Find the correct word(s) from the list below to complete each sentence.

   a The disadvantages of the current account are, that no ___ is earned and ___ may have to be paid.
   b Wages can be paid by employers using the ___ credit system.
   c Regular payments of a fixed amount from a current account can best be made using a ___
   d With direct debit the ___ requests payment.
   e A method of obtaining cash from a bank when it is closed is using ___
   f Shops are more willing to accept cheques if a ___ is also presented.

   List of words:
   charges, payee, cash dispensers, interest, giro, standing order, cheque guarantee card

4. Translate.

   a Wir haben gestern DM 50 000,00 auf Ihr Konto gutgeschrieben.
   b Wir bitten Sie, den Rechnungsbetrag an die Dresdner Bank, Frankfurt/M., Kontonummer 332 667 zu überweisen.
   c Wir haben unsere Bank beauftragt, den Betrag auf Ihr Konto bei der Deutschen Bank zu übertragen.
   d Wir bestätigen, Ihre Überweisung von DM 600,00 erhalten zu haben.

5. Which statement about the giro postal offices is not true?

   a Money transfers are possible between two postal giro accounts.
   b Remittances from a bank current account to a postal giro account cannot be effected.
   c There are no charges for money transfers between postal giro accounts.
   d Transfer of money from the postal giro account to the current account of a bank is possible.
   e The postal giro offices provide postal giro cheques for their customers.

EINRICHTUNGSHAUS
MATHÄUS

Teppiche, Bodenbeläge, Gardinen

Einrichtungshaus Mathäus, Burgstadtallee 73—75, 98701 Neustadt

Burgstadtalle 73-75
98701 Neustadt
Telefon: 09 87 / 21 12 11-2 13

Kontoverbindungen:
Sparkasse Neustadt
Konto-Nr. 34 246 109 (BLZ 987 564 32)
Postscheckamt Burgstadt
Konto-Nr. 175 215-K11 (BLZ 900 100 01)
Bankhaus Meyer & Co AG. Neustadt
Konto-Nr. 311 516 (BLZ 987 301 97)

Herrn
Markus Lambert
Kirchweg 18

99985 Berghausen

Datum 20.02.19. .

Rechnung

Rechnungs-Nr. 844

	DM	DM
Wir lieferten Ihnen Teppichboden Qualität 1 a		
12 m² pro m²	28,50	342,-
+ 15 % Mehrwertsteuer		51,30
		393,30

Vielen Dank für Ihren Auftrag
Bei Zahlung innerhalb von 10 Kalendertagen
gewähren wir 2 % Skonto.

Bitte bei Zahlungen und Schriftwechsel stets
die Rechnungs-Nummer mit angeben

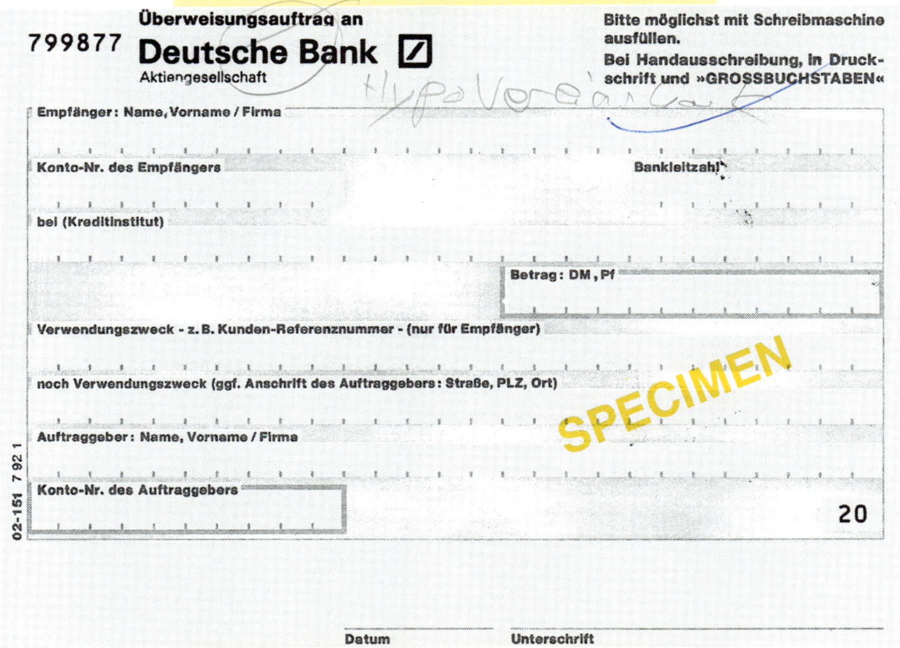
799877 Überweisungsauftrag an
Deutsche Bank
Aktiengesellschaft

Bitte möglichst mit Schreibmaschine ausfüllen.
Bei Handausschreibung, in Druckschrift und »GROSSBUCHSTABEN«

Empfänger: Name, Vorname / Firma
Konto-Nr. des Empfängers
Bankleitzahl
bei (Kreditinstitut)
Betrag: DM, Pf
Verwendungszweck - z. B. Kunden-Referenznummer - (nur für Empfänger)
noch Verwendungszweck (ggf. Anschrift des Auftraggebers: Straße, PLZ, Ort)
Auftraggeber: Name, Vorname / Firma
Konto-Nr. des Auftraggebers
20
02-151 7 92 1
Datum
Unterschrift

1. First, have a look at the invoice and answer the following questions in complete sentences.
   - **a** Who is the supplier? Einrichtungshaus Mathäus
   - **b** What does he supply? Some things to design a room
   - **c** What did Mr Lambert purchase? A carpet (Teppich)
   - **d** How much is the net price, VAT and the total?
   - **e** What are the conditions of payment?

2. Work with your partner and play the roles of a bank clerk and the customer who comes to the bank with this invoice to transfer the money.

   (Words you may need for the conversation: furniture, carpet, fitted carpet, curtain, to deliver, VAT = value added tax, square metre, order, to allow cash discount)

   The information given at the beginning of this chapter will help you to lead the conversation.

Dialogue: Standing order and direct debit system

An English speaking customer of your bank has had trouble with the owner of her flat because she forgot to transfer the rent twice. Tomorrow morning you will meet her in the bank to inform her about the standing order system.

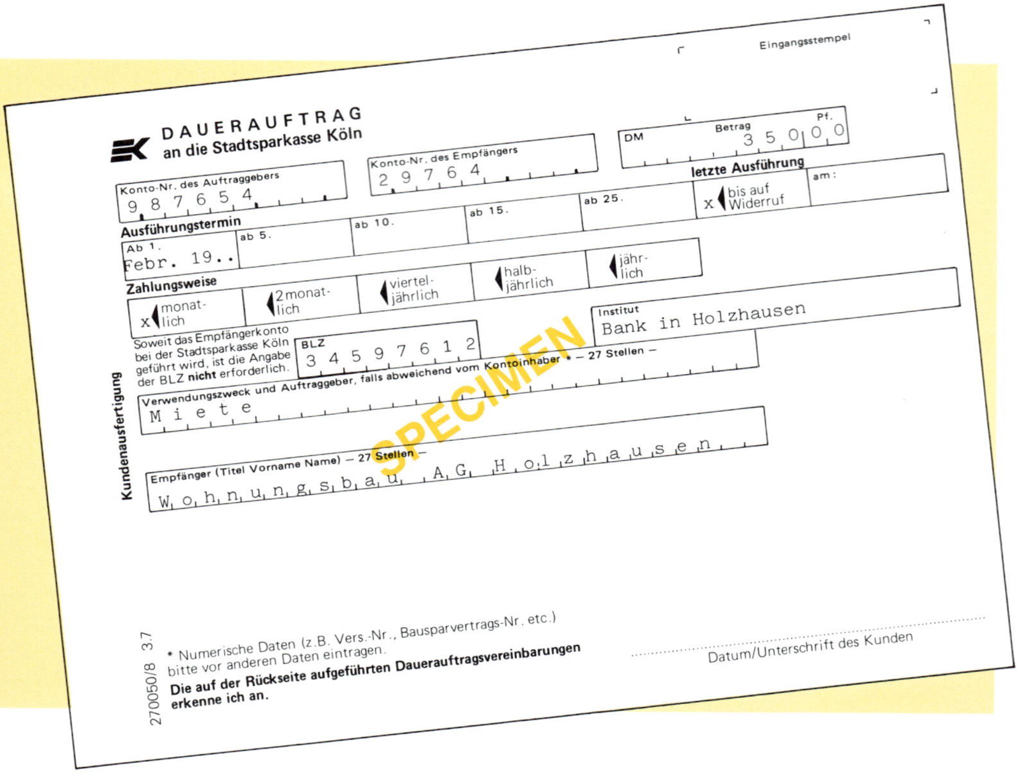

Eingangsstempel

DAUERAUFTRAG
an die Stadtsparkasse Köln

Konto-Nr. des Auftraggebers: 9 8 7 6 5 4

Konto-Nr. des Empfängers: 2 9 7 6 4

DM Betrag Pf.: 3 5 0 0 0

Ausführungstermin: Ab 1. Febr. 19.. | ab 5. | ab 10. | ab 15. | ab 25.

letzte Ausführung: x bis auf Widerruf | am:

Zahlungsweise: x monatlich | 2monatlich | vierteljährlich | halbjährlich | jährlich

Soweit das Empfängerkonto bei der Stadtsparkasse Köln geführt wird, ist die Angabe der BLZ **nicht** erforderlich.

BLZ: 3 4 5 9 7 6 1 2

Institut: Bank in Holzhausen

Verwendungszweck und Auftraggeber, falls abweichend vom Kontoinhaber * – 27 Stellen –

Miete

Empfänger (Titel Vorname Name) – 27 Stellen –

Wohnungsbau AG Holzhausen

SPECIMEN

Kundenausfertigung

* Numerische Daten (z.B. Vers.-Nr., Bausparvertrags-Nr. etc.) bitte vor anderen Daten eintragen.

Die auf der Rückseite aufgeführten Dauerauftragsvereinbarungen erkenne ich an.

Datum/Unterschrift des Kunden

270050/8 3.7

1. Make some notes about the standing order system to prepare yourself for the conversation tomorrow.

2. You were successful and the lady agreed to arrange a standing order for the rent. You see above the form for the standing order, already filled in.

   Now, work in pairs and simulate the dialogue that took place in order to fill in this standing order form. Ask and answer in complete sentences.

3. Some days later the lady comes to the bank with an authorization form asking for permission to debit her account for the amount of the bill she got from the gas company. She asks you to explain to her in English how the direct debit system works.

Listening: Making individual payments

Unit 5
Electronic banking

A bank's service hall of the year 2000

Part A

1 How do you think computers will influence banking?

2 Many changes in the services provided by banks are linked with electronic banking. Make sure that you understand the basic meaning of the following technical terms before you start with more detailed work.
Which of the English and German terms have a similar meaning? Be careful: a word-by-word translation is not possible with each item. Find the exact meaning of each of the terms by using English and German dictionaries.

English terms:	*German terms:*
A Cash dispenser	**a** Datenträgeraustausch
B Automatic teller machine	**b** Selbstbedienungsbank
C Exchange of data media	**c** Geldausgabeautomat
D Prestel	**d** Belegloser Zahlungsverkehr
E Electronic money transmission	**e** Bildschirmtext

Part B — Cash dispensers and ATMs

Increasing use of technology in the banks as well as the need to extend service beyond the basic 9.30 am to 15.30 pm banking hours has led to the development of automated machinery.
Initially this took the form of 'through the wall' cash dispensers. They were fixed to the outside wall of many banks. The earliest machines sometimes retained the customer's card.
Further research brought three major developments:

– more sophisticated cash dispensing,
– automatic account updating,
– extension of services.

The new generation of machines are, in fact, automated cashiers. These Automated Teller Machines or ATMs have now appeared not only 'through the wall' but also inside the service hall in an attempt to reduce queues at tills, and to free cashiers to deal with more individual queries and transactions.

"Lobby banking" provides fully automated areas to which customers gain access outside banking hours by inserting a special card into the door. Once inside, the customers can use their Cashpoint card. With all ATMs, customers are issued a card and an exclusive PIN (Personal Identification Number). After inserting the card and keying in the PIN the ATM will put a menu on the screen, listing all the services provided.

1 Find synonyms for the following words occurring in the text above.

a initially (line 5)
b retained (line 8)
c major (line 10)
d tills (line 20)
e sophisticated (line 12)
f updating (line 13)
g appeared (line 17)
h queries (line 21)
i access (line 23)
j keying in (line 29)

2 Answer these questions on the text.

a What was a big disadvantage of the early 'through the wall' cash dispenser?
b What is the positive effect of the new ATMs for both bank employees and customers?
c What kind of services are usually offered by 'Lobby Banking'?

Part C — Homebanking in Britain

For several years there has been talk of being able to transact 'banking' business from home, but despite the potential for such a system only two schemes have so far been set up.

One of these is run by the Nottingham Building Society in conjunction with the Bank of Scotland, the second by the Bank of Scotland itself. Both systems use Prestel to give customers access to the bank's computer.

Although the technology is available to provide 'homebanking', the services at present provided are limited. For example, the Bank of Scotland service provides

– payment of bills up to 30 days in advance,
– switching of funds to interest-earning accounts,
– viewing facility via TV of account transactions,
– cheque-book and statement ordering,
– cash management module for small businesses.

There is reluctance at present on the part of the Banks to move into the mass homebanking market. This is probably due to

– the fact that they have large branch networks,
– public indifference,
– security problems.

1 Look at these definitions of some key words from the text about 'homebanking'. Try to find the corresponding technical term.

a a business organization into which people pay money in order to save it and gain interest, and which lends money to people who want to buy houses
b a means for data communication using the telephone network and a TV set
c a list of things bought showing the total amount that must be paid
d money deposited in a bank with a high yield for the investor
e the art of controlling and dealing with money
f the divisions and parts of a large bank organisation

2 Prepare a short talk about the perspectives of homebanking in Germany. Give your opinion concerning the following questions.

a Is the necessary modern technology available?
b Are there possible advantages for the banks' customers?
c What kind of banks are inclined to support homebanking?
d Are there banks in Germany which have already introduced homebanking?

Part D

Look what your ATM card does for you!

Make Purchases

- Up to $1000 per day at participating merchants displaying the EXPLORE® symbol. Convenient locations all over California and throughout the West.

New· Check Cashing Identification

- Instant recognition and identification at Union Bank offices – beginning this Fall.

And that's not all! Your ATM card also gives you access to:

Call 1ST Banking information and service over the phone

Phone CALL 1ST 24 hours a day, 7 days a week. Simply by entering your Customer ID Number, secret code and the appropriate Action Code you can find out:

Service	Action Code
● Your account balance	*10#
● Your available Cash Reserve	*12#
● The status of a check	*13#
● Your last 4 deposits/credits	*15#
● Your last 4 checks recorded	*16#
● Your last 4 ATM transactions	*17#
● Current interest rates on CD's and other interest bearing accounts	
● Loan information – both the interest rate and approximate monthly payments for the most popular loans.	

Electronic banking services in Britain

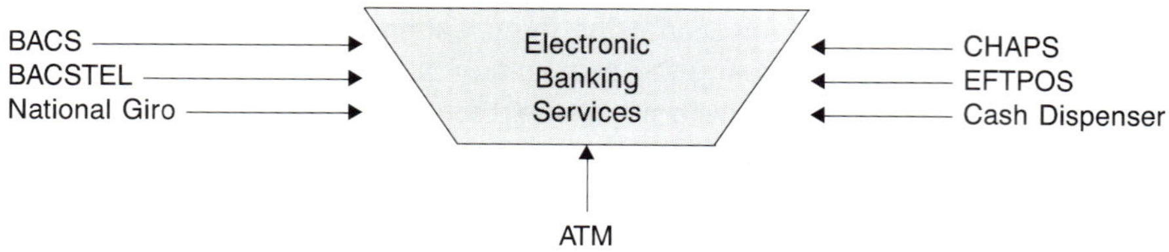

BACS: Bankers Automated Clearing Services
The aim of this service — set up in 1968 — is to replace sending vast amounts of paper by the electronic transfer of funds.

BACSTEL: BACS via a telephone
Data can be sent down the line by the user either at specific transmission lines or on an 'on demand' basis.

CHAPS: Clearing House Automated Payments System
This system — set up in 1984 — provides a fully automated transfer system between accounts in different banks and deals with remittances of £ 10,000.00 and over.

EFTPOS: Electronic Funds Transfer at the Point of Sale
The idea is that the use of computer terminals in stores and supermarkets would allow goods to be paid for by an automated transfer from the customer's account to that of the shop.

National Giro
This system was introduced 1968 to provide a cheap and efficient money transfer system for people who don't have a bank account. It is a national computerised system for postal account holders.

The diagram above and the additional texts provide information about some electronic banking services that have been introduced in England since 1968. Answer the following questions using the information given in the text and your own knowledge about electronic banking today.

1. Does 'National Giro' work in a way similar to the German 'Postgiro' system? Why do you think BACS was introduced in the same year as 'National Giro'?

2. With BACSTEL a telephone is used to send data. How do you think the transport of data is effected in the BACS system?

3. What is the possible advantage for customers having their accounts with banks linked with each other by the CHAPS system?

4. What kind of technical equipment do the partners in the EFTPOS system need? Write the technical terms missing in the sentences below on your own piece of paper.

   a The customer uses ___ instead of cash.
   b The retailer uses ___ instead of cash register.
   c The data are transmitted via a telephone line to ___.

Unit 6
Working with cheques and bills

Different types of cheques

Part A

There are different types of cheques. Can you work out the differences? What do the words mean in German?

– Eurocheques Euroscheck
– Open cheques Barscheck
– Travellers cheques Reisescheck
– Crossed cheques Verrechnungsscheck
– Bearer cheques Inhaberscheck
– Order cheques Orderscheck
– Blank cheques Blankoscheck

1. **The date.**
2. **The amount in figures.** Zahlen
3. **The name** of the person you are paying money to. payee
4. **The amount of money in words** – this is so that it would be difficult for anyone to alter your cheque.
5. **Your signature** – this must be the same as the specimen signature you wrote out when you opened your account – so you must advise the bank if you change your signature.
6. **The counterfoil.**

"Barclays" is a registered trademark and is used with the permission of Barclays Bank PLC.

Part B How you will benefit from using Eurocheques and Eurocheque Cards

A lady enters the branch of a bank and wants to have some information on Eurocheques and Eurocheque Cards.

Clerk: Guten Tag! Womit kann ich Ihnen helfen?

Lady: Oh, I'm sorry. I can't speak German very well. Would it be possible for you to speak English?

Clerk: Ah, yes, I see. Well, I don't think that I can speak English very well but I think it will be possible to help you.

Lady: Your English is really excellent! It's very kind of you to speak English. Well, I've come to your branch because I need a Eurocheque card.

Clerk: That's no problem if you have an account with our bank.

Lady: I opened an account in this branch six weeks ago. You know I started working here in the foreign trade department of a chemical firm and didn't know that having a Eurocheque card is so important in Germany. They don't accept my BarclayCard here in most shops.

Clerk: You are certainly right. Credit cards are not as widely accepted here as in Britain. For paying in shops you need Eurocheques and a Eurocheque card. When you want to pay, you first show your cheque card. Then you fill in and sign the cheque as usual in the presence of the retailer you are handing it to.

Lady: How does the person getting the cheque know that the cheque will be honoured?

Clerk: After he has seen you filling in and signing the cheque he will compare your signature on the cheque with the specimen on the cheque card, then he will compare the account number on the cheque with the one on the cheque card; after that he will examine the expiry date of the cheque card and make sure that the number of the cheque card has been written on the back of the cheque. Now he will be sure that the cheque can be cashed.

Lady: And if I want to stop payment?

Clerk: Once you have filled in and signed the cheque you cannot countermand payment. Even if the Eurocheque cardholder dies in the meantime the cheque will be paid.

Lady: And can I get cash at a bank?

Clerk: Yes, of course. Eurocheques can be cashed up to the guaranteed amount. But if you pay a small extra fee you can use your Eurocheque card with cash dispensers, too.

Lady: That's really very favourable. I didn't know that.
But please tell me – can I get cash abroad, too?

Clerk: Sure. You can obtain cash in almost all European and Mediterranean countries.

Lady: Well, I'd like to apply for that card. What has to be done?

Clerk: Please let me have your account number first, then …

1 Give answers and explanations.

a Why do shops, hotels and the like not have to worry about cheques issued in connection with a cheque card?
b Explain how to use the Eurocheque card.
c How do you use your Eurocheques in countries outside Germany?
d What criteria do you think banks use to decide which customers get a Eurocheque card?
e Why is the expiry date so important?
f Find another expression for "to countermand" payment.
g Do all shops in Europe accept Eurocheques?
h Can you stop payment of a Eurocheque that has been filled in and signed?
i Where can you get cash – at home and abroad – by using Eurocheques and/or Eurocheque card?
j Why is this method of payment so convenient?

2 Say it in English: Using Eurocheques

a Sie können jederzeit Bargeld bekommen, wenn Sie einen Euroscheck und eine Scheckkarte besitzen.
b Die Scheckkarte garantiert die Einlösung jedes Schecks bis zu einem Gegenwert von annähernd 400,00 DM.
c Der Euroscheck kann in der jeweiligen Landeswährung ausgestellt werden.
d Der Empfänger des Euroschecks muß prüfen, ob auch die Scheckkarte noch gültig ist.
e Sogar bei Bargeldautomaten kann die Scheckkarte benutzt werden.
f Sie brauchen sich um die Einlösung des Schecks keine Sorgen machen.
g Achten Sie auf das Eurocheque-Zeichen; dort können sie mit Euroscheck zahlen bzw. Geld erhalten.
h Auch wenn der Aussteller in der Zwischenzeit stirbt, wird der Euroscheck eingelöst.
i In ganz Europa kann man mit Euroschecks genauso leicht wie mit Bargeld bezahlen.
j Eine Liste aller Banken, die auch außerhalb Europas Euroschecks akzeptieren sowie weitere Informationen sind in unserer Niederlassung erhältlich.

Part C

Further information on the different types of cheques

What is a cheque? In very simple terms a cheque is an order signed by a customer, addressed to his or her bank, to pay the amount indicated to the person(s) or company named. **Open cheques** can only be cashed at the drawee's bank. Customers give them to someone they want to pay. The standard practice of writing the amount on the cheques in words and figures does not extend to the Pfennige. These can be written in figures. Because it's an open cheque, the payee could, if he wished, take it to the drawee's bank and obtain cash.

Eurocheques, if accompanied by a cheque card, can be cashed at every bank in Germany and Europe displaying the EC symbol.

If you do not want cheques to be paid in cash you'd better use **crossed cheques.** They have two parallel lines on them and must be paid into an account. This means they are much safer, and the recipient can always be traced back; and the risk of loss or theft is lessened.

Bearer cheques can be negotiated (i.e. transferred or passed on) like a bank note. The most common form of a bearer cheque is the Eurocheque.

Order cheques are payable to a named person or to his/her order. They can only be negotiated by endorsement.

Travellers' cheques are issued in certain currencies by banks to customers wishing to travel abroad. Each cheque has a space for him to sign as soon as he gets the cheques, and another space for him to sign in the presence of the person accepting the cheque. If the customer loses them or if they are stolen through no fault of his own, the bank, when notified, will usually replace them free of charge.

Cheques where the amount has not been filled in are called "blank cheques".

1 Ask your partner about the different types of cheques. Work in pairs.

2 Complete the following sentences by inserting the appropriate word from the list below. Write your answers on a separate piece of paper.

selected; leaflet; equivalent; touch; specimen; currency; authorize; convenient; liable; property; locations; pay out

- **a** The signature on the cheque has to be compared with the ___ on the cheque card.
- **b** The card remains the ___ of the issuing bank at all times.
- **c** You can use your cheque to withdraw the ___ of approximately £ 100.00.
- **d** The network is soon to be expanded to 10,000 machines in 19 countries, making local ___ available 24 hours per day at the ___ of a button.
- **e** A full list of the current ___ is available in our directory.
- **f** Eurocheques complement our extensive travel service by providing a ___ method of using cheques at banks.
- **g** To fill in a cheque is to ___ the bank to ___ money from your account.
- **h** Eurocheques can be cashed at ___ banks in countries outside Germany.
- **i** The issuing bank shall not be ___ for any Eurocheque that has been filled in and signed even if the cardholder dies in the meantime.
- **j** A list of all the banks where you can obtain cash and other useful information is printed in our ___ which you may get from any of our branches.

Discount credit

Discount credit arises as a result of the buying, i.e. advance lending, of claims based on bills. The interest is calculated in advance and is deducted from the bill amount as a discount. The actual amount loaned is, therefore, not the nominal value but the cash value of the bill. In law the discounting of a bill is not lending but a purchase.

The bank reserves the right to buy only properly made-out bills. Even bills that have already been discounted can be given back if there is something disadvantageous about any of the parties to it (drawer, drawee, presenter). Only bills of impeccable creditworthiness can be rediscounted and thereby form part of the liquid reserves of the bank.

Taken primarily from the point of view of creditworthiness, there are three categories of bills in the bill discount business:

Trade bills are bills arising from trading. The drawee has, therefore, acquired physical items that can be processed or resold. They offer a certain security for the bill, because their proceeds are normally sufficient to cover the bill.

Finance bills are only used to raise loans. There is no debt relationship based on physical goods or services to back it up. Its creditworthiness must, therefore, be assessed with more care.

Private discounts are first-class bank acceptances used to finance foreign trade. They are handled by the banks as a means of depositing money. The discount rate can be lower than at the Bundesbank, but in recent years it was mostly higher.

For the most part discount transactions at the banks are based on genuine trade bills. As long as they are recognized as such, finance bills are calculated at a higher discount rate. As the Bundesbank does not normally buy them, the distinction between trade and finance bills is especially important.

- Make a short speech about discount credits according to the information given in the text above. The following questions can help you to prepare an adequate speech.

  a Is discounting a bill a result of lending money or buying a claim?
  b How are the nominal value and the cash value of bills distinguished from each other?
  c How are the parties called who are involved in the business of discount credit?
  d Which categories of bills are there from the point of view of creditworthiness?
  e Why is the distinction between trade and finance bills important?

Listening

Text One: Drawing cheques

Text Two: Presenting cheques

Text Three: Informing the bank about last cheques

Unit 7
Foreign travel services

Part A

How to take your money abroad

Country	Currency	Travellers Cheques Recommended Currency	Eurocheques Acceptance Grade Bank	Retailer	Credit Cards Acceptance Grade Bank	Retailer
Austria	Schilling	Sterling	A	A	B	B
France	French Franc	French Franc	A	A	A	A
Germany	Deutschmark	Deutschmark	A	A	A	A
Greece	Drachma	Sterling	A	B	A	A
Israel	New Sheqel	Sterling	A	C	A	A
Italy	Lire	Lire	A	A	A	A
Japan	Yen	Yen	–	–	A	A
Netherlands	Guilder	Guilder	A	A	B	B
Portugal	Escudo	Escudo	A	A	A	A
Russia	Rouble	Sterling	A	C	–	B
Spain	Peseta	Peseta	A	A	A	A
Switzerland	Swiss Franc	Swiss Franc	A	A	A	A
Turkey	Lirasi	Sterling	A	C	B	B
USA	US Dollar	US Dollar	–	–	A	A

Key: Eurocheque and Credit Cards ▶ A. Widely accepted
B. Only in tourist areas
C. Limited Service

Look at the chart above.

1. Which countries don't accept Eurocheques? Can you think of a reason why they don't?
2. In which countries would you have trouble using your credit cards?
3. What do you think is the best way to take your money abroad?
4. How can you protect yourself in case your money is stolen in a foreign country?
5. What other factors should be taken into consideration if you're planning to take a trip abroad?

Whether it's for business or pleasure, travelling abroad can sometimes seem rather hard work. There are so many things to think of – tickets, passports, sometimes even visas to organise. Then there are those anxious hours as departure time approaches. Have you packed everything? Will you get to the station, airport or ferry terminal on time? With all these things to occupy you, it's easy to overlook one of the most essential ingredients of a good trip: money. You could easily find yourself in a country without the correct local currency or without the right insurance to cover you or your car. Things like this can ruin even the best travel plans. Believe it or not, your bank can be the place to go to find a solution, as many banks nowadays offer comprehensive travel services.

What you'll need

These days there are so many different ways to take money abroad, it can be difficult deciding which is best for your situation. Usually it's a combination of things. Some cash, of course. Some readily exchangeable cheques for the cash you'll need during your stay. And, perhaps, a back-up to pay for any unexpected bills – or extravagant presents.

Foreign Currency

Wherever you're going, you are likely to need some foreign currency. There will be taxi fares to pay, porters to tip and of course the odd meal or drink before you reach your final destination. And if you're travelling on the weekend, don't forget the local banks won't be open until Monday morning.

Travellers Cheques

Even if you're going to a country that accepts Eurocheques as well as major credit cards (Access, Visa, American Express, Barclaycard), it's still worth taking travellers cheques, too. After all, if you ever lose your travellers cheques, they can always be refunded. Travellers cheques are available in most major currencies. If you take cheques in the currency of your destination, you are likely to get a better rate of exchange and avoid any excess commission that may be charged in some countries. Any unused cheques can be retained for your next trip or sold back to the bank.

Travel Insurance

It's important to take out insurance well before setting off abroad to take care of problems which can arise such as becoming ill, losing your money or having your luggage lost. For a small premium the travel insurance can carry the risk and you can enjoy your holiday to the full, knowing that if something does go wrong, it's not you who foots the bill.

Many banks offer comprehensive insurance packages designed for people travelling abroad both with and without their cars. Here is an example of the coverage offered by Barclays Bank as well as the premiums charged.

The benefits

Cover		
Medical expenses	Unlimited*	If you become ill, or have an accident.
Additional hospital benefit	Up to £200	If you are admitted to hospital as an in-patient outside the UK.
Cancellation charges	Up to £1,500*	If you have to cancel or cut short your holiday for a variety of reasons, you can claim reimbursement.
Personal property	£1,000* in all	If anything is stolen or damaged. There is a single article limit of £200 and an overall limit of £200 for jewellery and photographic equipment.
including Baggage delay	up to £50	For luggage temporarily mislaid for more than 12 hours in transit.
and also including Money	Up to £200*	For loss of your money, your travellers cheques or your tickets.
Personal liability	Up to £500,000	For your legal liability in respect of third party damage or injury claims against you.
Travel delay	Up to £60	If your boat or plane is delayed for more than 12 hours.
Failure of public transport	Up to £150	For additional travel and hotel expenses arising from failure of public scheduled transport.
Personal accident	Up to £15,000	In the event of death or permanent disablement, or loss of limb(s) or eye(s)
Emergency medical assistance	'24 hour'	A 24 hour emergency medical assistance service.

* Each person must pay the first £25 of each claim.

The cost

Period	Up to 8 days £	9–12 days £	13–17 days £	18–24 days £	25–31 days £	Add for each extra week up to 6 months (£)
Area 1 UK	3.65	4.05	4.95	5.75	6.60	1.05
Area 2 Europe	11.20	12.10	13.20	14.50	15.70	3.50
Area 3 World-wide	35.85	35.85	35.85	40.45	45.05	10.00

(Barclays Bank)

1 Decide whether the following statements are true or false.

a Unused travellers cheques can only be cashed in the country the currency of which they are issued in.
b Travel insurance is usually an expensive luxury.
c Banks today sell travel insurance policies.
d If you have credit cards, it is not necessary to carry Eurocheques or travellers cheques.
e A travel insurance policy will reimburse you if you have spent an extra night in a city because a scheduled train or bus was late or cancelled.
f Pensioners must pay higher premiums for travel insurance if they go to the U.S.A. or Asia.

2 Answer the questions according to the information in the texts.

a Why is it a good idea to take some of the local currency with you and not wait to change all your money when you arrive?
b What are the advantages of travellers cheques?
c What is the advantage of buying travellers cheques in the currency of the country you are visiting?
d Besides foreign currency what other travel services do banks offer?
e What risks can be eliminated by having a travel insurance policy?

3 Which words are synonyms or synonymous expressions?

Column A	*Column B*
A essential	**a** to keep busy
B comprehensive	**b** components
C extravagant	**c** fee charged for changing money
D commission	**d** necessary
E abroad	**e** inclusive
F to occupy someone	**f** cost of an insurance policy
G ingredients	**g** very expensive
H premium	**h** in foreign countries

4 Complete the following sentences.

a If you are planning a trip abroad, ___
b If you don't organise things well, ___
c If you arrive in a country on the weekend, ___
d If you lose your travellers cheques, ___
e If you have an accident while driving a car in a foreign country, ___
f If your luggage is lost, ___
g If your plane is delayed for more than 12 hours, ___

5 Add prepositions.

a Travellers cheques can be bought ___ most major currencies.
b Before setting ___ on a journey you should take ___ a travel insurance policy.
c Good planning is essential because there are so many things to think ___
d A Barclays Bank Travel Insurance Policy will pay up to £15,000.00 ___ the event ___ death.

Document: Travel Services Request Form

Travel Services Request Form

To: Lloyds Bank Plc

Name of traveller (who should sign the Travellers Cheques): ______________________

I wish to collect my travel facilities on (date): ______________________

Sterling Travellers Cheques

Please supply me with £ ______ of Sterling travellers cheques.

Please write in the appropriate box how many of each pre-prepared pack you require.

	£10 cheques	£20 cheques	£50 cheques	£100 cheques
3 cheque pack	£30	£60	£150	£300
5 cheque pack	£50	£100	£250	£500
10 cheque pack		£200	£500	

Foreign Currency Notes

for use in	currency amount	sterling equivalent
		or £
		or £
		or £

SPECIMEN

Foreign Currency Travellers Cheques

for use in	currency amount	sterling equivalent
		or £
		or £
		or £

US$ travellers cheques are supplied in pre-prepared packs and we will try to meet your requirements as closely as possible. If you have a preference for one or more denominations please tick the appropriate box(es). US$20 ☐ US$50 ☐ US$100 ☐ US$500 ☐

The terms and conditions of sale which apply to Travellers Cheques are those of the issuing institution for which Lloyds Bank Plc is acting as agent.

Currency Notes and Currency Travellers Cheques The cost of currency notes and currency travellers cheques will be calculated as follows:

1. If held in stock at the issuing branch – using the rate of exchange at that branch on the date the facilities are stated to be required.
2. If NOT held in stock at the issuing branch – using the rate of exchange ruling at the Bank's International Banking Division on the date the facilities are sent to this branch.

Lloyds Bank Travel Insurance

I/We require travel insurance as indicated on the application form opposite.

I/We will pay the cost plus charges for the above by *cash/cheque/Access cash advance.

*Please debit my/our account at (Lloyds Branch):

** Delete as applicable*

My/our account number is: ☐☐☐☐☐☐☐☐

Signature(s) ______________________ Date ______________

Address (if not a customer): ______________________

______________________ Postcode ______________

Lloyds Bank Uniform Eurocheques

These can be used just like your ordinary cheques and Cheque Card wherever you see the 'EC' symbol. Please tick the box if you would like to receive a leaflet and application form. ☐

FOR BANK USE ONLY

Issue Number

Currency and/or Currency T/C's ordered

Date:

Initials:

£

£

£

£

TOTAL COST

£

(Lloyds Bank)

- On a separate piece of paper list the information you would need to fill in the Travel Services Request Form above.

Listening: Travellers' cheques

Unit 8
More comfort with credit cards?

What do you know about credit cards?

Part A

1. What do these stickers mean?
2. Can you use all the cards for the same purpose?
3. Is there any difference between an American Express Card and a Visa Card?
4. When are these cards used?
5. Do you have any of these cards?
6. Can you think of any advantages of having such cards?

Credit cards compared to travel and entertainment cards

Part B

The term 'credit card' is generally used for all plastic cards that can be used as money. However, this is not very accurate. There are actually two kinds of plastic cards in use: 'credit cards' and 'travel and entertainment cards'. What is the difference? This can be explained by looking at the definitions of the word "credit". On the one hand, credit refers to a system of buying goods or services and paying for them later, often by means of installments*. In this sense the VISA CARD and MASTERCARD (known in Britain as the BARCLAYCARD and ACCESS CARD) are credit cards. On the other hand, credit also means the amount of money a bank or finance company places at a client's disposal and which he can draw upon. Again, the cards already mentioned qualify as credit cards.

When the monthly statement arrives, the cardholder can decide whether to pay his bill in full or to pay only part of it. If he decides to pay the total bill, there is no finance charge. If, however, the cardholder chooses to pay in installments, he must pay at least the minimum shown on the statement in the space labeled Installment Payment. He may, of course, choose to pay more than the minimum. In any case, the credit card company will charge a finance charge on the unpaid balance. In addition to the finance charge, most credit card companies require their cardholders to pay an annual fee for the privilege of being allowed to use the company's card.

In contrast to the 'credit card', all charges made on a 'travel and entertainment card' must be paid in full within a period specified on the statement. Since the card-issuing company doesn't actually extend 'credit', the cardholder doesn't ever have to pay a finance charge, and there is often no limit to the amount he can 'charge' to his card. Both, the American Express Card and the Diner's Club Card are travel and entertainment cards. American Express, however, does make it possible for its cardmembers to pay for airline tickets in installments, but this must be arranged at the time of purchase. Both types of card issuing companies charge the participating business establishments a fee for their service.

Regardless of which type of card is used, a sales voucher containing all information pertinent to the transaction is filled out at the time of purchase. There are usually three copies of this voucher, one for the customer, one for the establishment and one for the credit card company. Once a month the cardholder receives a statement listing all purchases and payments made during the billing period as well as any finance charges.

* American English: installment, British English: instalment

Information given by American Express

Apply for the world's most respected Card.

When you picked up this American Express Card application, you made a wise decision – to become a Cardmember and enjoy the exclusive privileges of the Card.

What better way to make your active life easier. When you travel, shop or entertain – the Card will bring you an extra measure of security and convenience ...

A welcome companion at home and around the globe. More than 300 airlines, and most major car rentals, fine restaurants, hotels, department and specialty stores all welcome the Card. So there's no need to carry large amounts of cash.

A helping hand when traveling. Over 1,200 Travel Service Offices* are your worldwide "homes away from home." They help with travel plans and with emergencies. And if the Card is lost or stolen, they usually replace it the next business day.

Financial freedom. There is no spending limit set in advance. You're limited only by your ability to pay, based upon the spending and payment patterns you establish as you use the Card and your personal resources. So you have maximum control of your finances.

Personal checks guaranteed. For up to $1,000 at most American Express* Travel Service Offices (up to $200 in local currency, the rest in American Express Travelers Cheques). For up to $250 at most hotels and motels in the U.S. and Canada (up to $100 elsewhere). These services are subject to cash availability and local regulations.

Personal service. Whether we're providing signed copies of charges for easy recordkeeping or toll-free customer service, you can count on American Express for attentive assistance.

The American Express Card. Designed to suit your lifestyle. Apply today.

Inquire about the Corporate Card Program for company management and control of travel expenses. Call toll-free, 1-800-528-2122.

* Offices of American Express Travel Related Services Company. Inc., its affiliates and Representatives

(American Express)

1 True or false?

If a statement is true, cite the appropriate passage in the text that supports your judgment. If it is false, change it so that it agrees with the text.

a All credit cards are basically the same.
b If you receive credit, you must always pay the total amount at once.
c Only business establishments pay a finance charge.
d If you lose a sales voucher, there is no way of establishing exactly how much a purchase amounted to.
e There is no advantage in paying a VISA bill in full.
f An American Express Card can't be used outside the United States.
g Having a credit card means it's unnecessary to carry large amounts of cash when you travel.

2 Make questions for the following answers.

a the BARCLAYCARD
b the monthly statement
c a travel and entertainment card
d yearly fee
e three

3 Put the following statements in the same order as they occur in the text "Information given by American Express".

a If you lose your American Express Card, it can be replaced very quickly.
b Cardmembers receive copies of all charges, which makes it easy to keep track of financial transactions.
c The American Express Card is accepted by many airlines all over the world.
d You can call American Express without being charged for the phone call.
e American Express Travel Service Offices usually provide a cheque-cashing service for cardmembers.

4 Which expressions from the text (column B) correspond to the explanations on column A?

Column A	*Column B*
A to make use of a supply (usually money)	**a** by means of
B to settle an account	**b** to place at someone's disposal
C to make available for someone to use	**c** in contrast to
D by using something	**d** to pay in full
E to enable someone to do something	**e** in addition to
F by comparison	**f** to make it possible for someone to do something
G moreover	**g** to draw upon/on

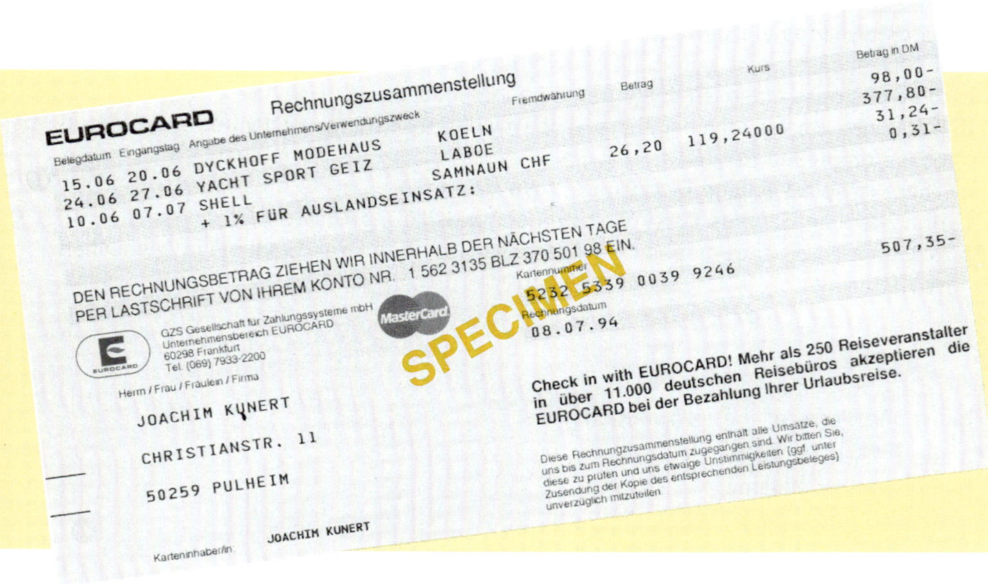
EUROCARD Rechnungszusammenstellung

Belegdatum	Eingangstag	Angabe des Unternehmens/Verwendungszweck		Fremdwährung	Betrag	Kurs	Betrag in DM
15.06	20.06	DYCKHOFF MODEHAUS	KOELN				98,00-
24.06	27.06	YACHT SPORT GEIZ	LABOE				377,80-
10.06	07.07	SHELL	SAMNAUN	CHF	26,20	119,24000	31,24-
		+ 1% FÜR AUSLANDSEINSATZ:					0,31-

DEN RECHNUNGSBETRAG ZIEHEN WIR INNERHALB DER NÄCHSTEN TAGE PER LASTSCHRIFT VON IHREM KONTO NR. 1 562 3135 BLZ 370 501 98 EIN. 507,35-

Kartennummer 5232 5339 0039 9246

Rechnungsdatum 08.07.94

GZS Gesellschaft für Zahlungssysteme mbH
Unternehmensbereich EUROCARD
60298 Frankfurt
Tel. (069) 7933-2200

MasterCard

SPECIMEN

Herrn / Frau / Fräulein / Firma

JOACHIM KUNERT
CHRISTIANSTR. 11
50259 PULHEIM

Check in with EUROCARD! Mehr als 250 Reiseveranstalter in über 11.000 deutschen Reisebüros akzeptieren die EUROCARD bei der Bezahlung Ihrer Urlaubsreise.

Diese Rechnungzusammenstellung enthält alle Umsätze, die uns bis zum Rechnungsdatum zugegangen sind. Wir bitten Sie, diese zu prüfen und uns etwaige Unstimmigkeiten (ggf. unter Zusendung der Kopie des entsprechenden Leistungsbeleges) unverzüglich mitzuteilen.

Karteninhaber/in: JOACHIM KUNERT

Find the numbers from the sales slip and monthly statement, and write them on a separate piece of paper:

1. cardholder's account number
2. telephone number of Eurocard's agency in Germany
3. date of the bills
4. total amount of purchase during the period of the statement
5. closing date of statement
6. the last month the card is valid
7. names of the shops of purchase
8. manner of payment
9. identification number of the shop on the sales slip
10. date of the sales slip
11. amount of purchase on the sales slip
12. number of the sales slip
13. complete number of the credit card

14 amount of purchase in dollars

15 date payment is due

16 amount of credit still available

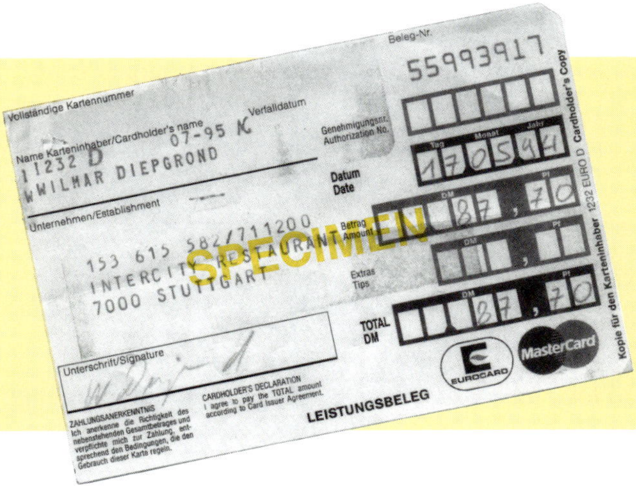

Letter: Applying for a credit card

Part D

Write a letter to a friend and try to convince him to apply for a credit card. Include the following information:

- the advantages of having a credit card,
- the difference between the two types of cards generally available,
- an account of a personal experience in which a credit card was useful to you,
- how to apply for one.

Listening: Credit Cards

Part E

Unit 9
Personal borrowing

Part A — A very good offer – but where to get the money from?

On his way home, John Saunders passes a furniture shop and reads the following poster:

Exclusively for members of the US army

Wouldn't you love to live in a comfortably furnished home like the one you had back home in the States?

We can help you with our extensive and complete range of fittings. Naturally we guarantee first-class quality and super low prices!

30–40 % off

We sell approx. 30–40 % below prices recommended by manufacturers. Additionally you'll get the 15 % German VAT refunded.

No extra charges for assembly and delivery!
We offer you 20 furnishing centers and more than 100,000 m² sales area. We are one of the largest furniture suppliers and are well-known.

- Living room furniture
- Sofas and matching chairs
- Bedroom furniture
- Children's and youth rooms
- Kitchens

Our friendly sales staff will advise you
in your own language – in English.
Come and see us!
Always worth a visit.

Asking for a personal loan

John Saunders (J. S.) wants to buy new furniture. But he doesn't have enough cash. So he phones his bank.

M. H. Stadtsparkasse Erlangen, Monika Hertlein.

J. S. Good afternoon, Frau Hertlein, would you mind if I speak English?

M. H. No, I don't. What can I do for you?

J. S. You see I have been here in Erlangen for only two weeks. On my way home I saw a very favourable offer for living room furniture. I need new armchairs and a new couch for my flat. I opened an account with your bank last week. But I don't know if there is enough money on my account because I'm waiting for a remittance. Will you be so kind and look up my current account balance, please?

M. H. I can understand your problem very well. But I have to tell you that I am not allowed to inform you about the balance by phone. It would be better if you came to our branch. Today we are open for another two hours.

J. S. That means you cannot tell me the balance of my account? That's strange! But if there is no other possibility I will come and see you immediately. Can I meet you in about an hour?

M. H. Yes, you can. If you tell me your name I can prepare all the necessary forms in case you need a credit.

J. S. That's very kind of you. My name is John Saunders.

M. H. Would you please spell your surname, Mr Saunders.

J. S. Yes, of course. Sugar – Able – Uncle – Nan – Dog – Easy – Roger – Sugar.

M. H. O.K. I hope I've got it, Mr Saunders. By the way, can you give me your account number, please. I need it to look up your balance.

J. S. Of course I can. It is 463 822. Have you got it?

M. H. Yes, I have. Thank you, Mr Saunders. See you in an hour.

J. S. Good bye, then. See you later.

One hour later John Saunders meets Monika Hertlein in her office.

M. H. Good afternoon, Mr Saunders. It's very kind of you to come here to our branch. Will you please sit down over there.

J. S. Thank you very much, Frau Hertlein. Well, did you find out if the remittance I'm waiting for has already been credited to my account?

M. H. Well, Mr Saunders, your remittance has not yet arrived. There are now 348.00 Deutschmarks in your account. But it will be no problem for us to grant you a personal loan.

J. S. I need about 2,000.00 Deutschmarks as a credit. How much will it cost?

M. H. Our interest rates are very competitive and throughout the term of the loan they are fixed. At present our rate of interest is 8 1/2 per cent.

J. S. Well, that's a reasonable rate. When do I have to pay the money back?

M. H. Loans are usually repaid by regular instalments, but you can also repay the loan in one sum at the end of the lending period.

J. S. I'd prefer regular instalments. That means I will apply for this loan.

M. H. Thank you very much for your quick decision, Mr Saunders. What you have to do now is to fill in this application form here.

J. S. O.K. I will complete it and send it back by Tuesday next week.

M. H. That's fine. If you need any help don't hesitate and call at our branch.

J. S. Thank you so much for your help. But I have to leave now. See you next week.

M. H. Good bye, Mr Saunders. Have a good afternoon.

Answer the following questions.

1. Why does Mr Saunders ask for a personal loan?
2. What is the difference between a personal loan and an overdraft?
3. Can you tell your customers all about the costs of a personal loan? Why would you recommend a personal loan?
4. How are loans made available to customers?
5. What are the advantages of a personal loan?
6. What do customers have to do to get a personal loan?
7. What will banks do, after customers have applied for a loan or an overdraft?
8. What does "VAT" mean?
9. Can you explain the phrase "Additionally you'll get the 15 % German VAT refunded"?

Part C

Loans and overdraft credits

Banks must always keep in mind two important principles:
First, they're lending other people's money, which they have to repay on demand; second, they're in business to make a profit.
Lending is principally by (a) overdraft, (b) loan and (c) personal loan.
An **overdraft** is an agreed limit borrowed on current accounts and the agreement that the amount lent will be repaid at a specific date. The interest is calculated daily and expressed as a percentage of the bank's base rate. Repayments are not meant to be regular. The overdraft may also be reduced by transfers, deposits or cash of cheques of the account holder or any other person. Interest is charged quarterly or half-yearly. A separate credit commission may be charged.
A **loan account** is separate from the customer's current account. The amount agreed is transferred to the current account, with an agreement on the part of the customer to repay by regular monthly instalments or in one sum at the end of the period. Transfers are usually made by standing orders. Interest is calculated on a daily basis and is fixed for the whole period or may vary as is the case with overdrafts. Interest is debited quarterly to the

customer's current account or at any other option of the customer.

Personal loans are given for the purchase of durable consumer goods, e.g. cars, furniture, video recorders, computers etc. Personal loans are usually made available for sums up to DM 30,000.00. These loans are repayable in equal monthly instalments of principal and interest over a period of six months to 60 months. Unlike a hire purchase agreement, the ownership of the property is with the purchaser/customer. The rate of interest is fixed when the loan is given, and this amount is added to the loan, so the customer knows exactly how much he owes and by agreement knows the period of the loan. Security is not normally required, sometimes assignment of claims or wages or liability of the customer's spouse is required. Consequently the rate of interest charged is slightly higher. Additionally a form of insurance is built into the loan condition.

1 Answer the following questions.

- **a** When does an overdraft occur?
- **b** What does the expression "going into the red" mean and where does it come from?
- **c** Explain the differences between loans and overdrafts.
- **d** What securities are required for personal loans?
- **e** In which way can overdrafts be repaid?
- **f** What do you think the bank's "principles of lending" are?
- **g** List the various ways interest is charged.
- **h** Why may personal loans be preferred by customers? Why not?

2 With your partner, play the parts of a bank clerk and a customer who asks for an advance. The following questions may help you.

- **a** What is the purpose of the advance?
- **b** How much is required?
- **c** How long is it wanted for?
- **d** What is the source of repayment?
- **e** How much interest is charged?

3 An American customer enters your branch and turns to your counter. He asks for a Personal Loan of 20,000.00 German marks for the purchase of a car. He has been employed by a big firm in Erlangen for five years. His net monthly income is 5,000.00 German marks and his regular monthly expenditure is 3,500.00 German marks.

Work out a dialogue between him and a banker. Consider the following circumstances:

- **a** Your monthly rate of interest is ___ %.
- **b** Service charge of ___ %.
- **c** Work out a repayment scheme. (Where should it be debited?)
- **d** Remember how long the customer has been employed.
- **e** Think of the various types of securities. What seems to be the best in this case?
- **f** Get an application form from your bank and ask for all the necessary details.

Listening: Overdrafts and Personal Loans

Security on loans

The security on loans is first of all based on the creditworthiness of the customer himself. Additional security rests either on joint liability through other parties or on the value of certain objects or claims that the borrower assigns or pledges to his bank.

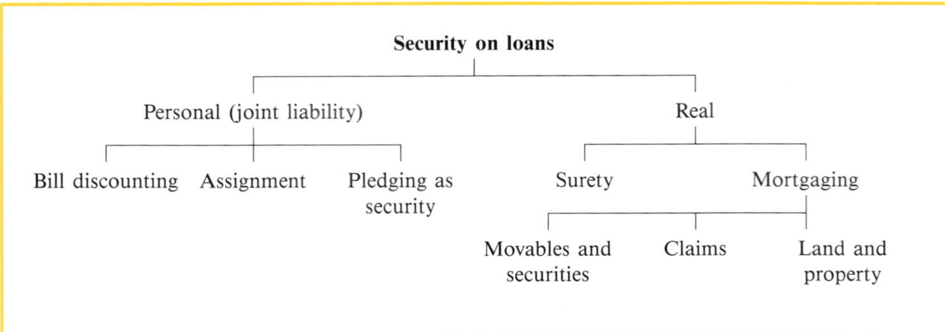

Surety

Whoever takes on a surety, pledges himself to the creditor of a third party (the borrower) to fulfill the payment of any liability arising. Such surety is a one-sided liability agreement that is made between the creditor and the guarantor without the participation of the debtor.

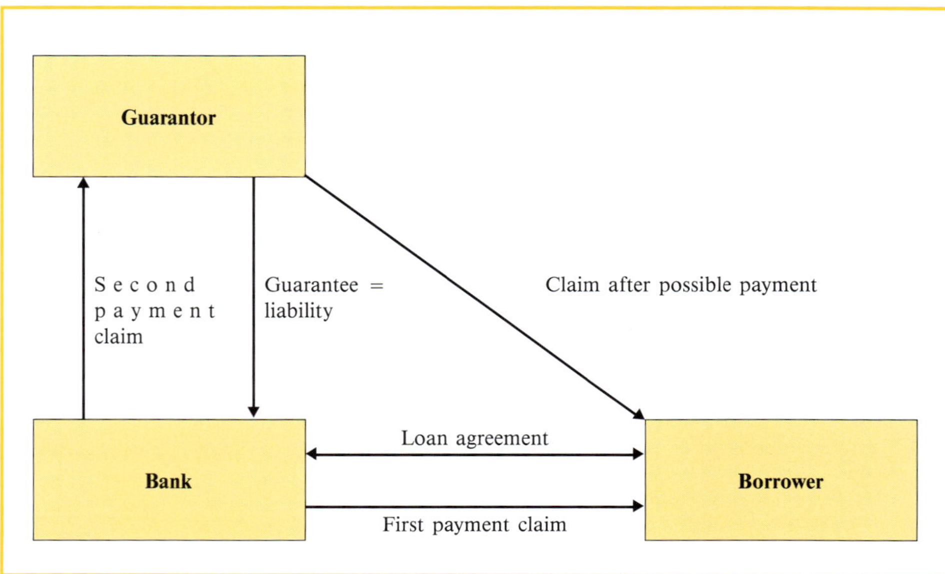

Assignment

Assignment of claims as security

Assignment of a transfer (surrender) of a claim by a creditor to a third party. If it is a contract bound by an agreement to secure a bank loan, the bank assumes the role of the creditor (the assignor), even when the debtor – now called the third-party debtor – does not know anything of this handover.

Liens

If a liability is secured by a lien in the form of a physical object, the creditor can in the case of default on payment redeem his claim by selling off the lien.

Claims and physical items can be held in lien. Movable objects are regarded as dead pledges in a lien, while land on the other hand is mortgaged via a mortgage lien (encumbrances).

Mortgage liens

The most stable security in terms of value for a bank loan are pledges in the form of land and property. They are not only used for long-term real estate loans, but also are frequently used for overdrafts. As land cannot be transferred, the lien is transferred into a public register, the land register.

Mortgages

A mortgage is a lien on a piece of land to secure a claim. It forms a valid contractual obligation, with which it is inextricably linked. The amount of the claim also determines the extent of the lien.

Land charges and annuity charges

In contrast to a mortgage, a land charge is a pledging of land which does not form a claim. It contains the abstract obligation, i.e. one not linked to the creation of the debt, to pay a certain sum from the piece of land. No individual is held responsible for a land charge, only the land itself is the debt (real debt).

1 There are a lot of technical terms in the texts above. Find out from the context which English terms correspond with these German expressions:

a akzessorisch verbunden,
b bewegliche Sachen,
c Bürge,
d Bürgschaft,
e Faustpfand,
f Forderung,
g Forderungsübertragung,
h Gläubiger,
i Grundbuch,
j Grundschuld,
k Grundstücksbelastung,
l Hypothek,
m Mithaftung,
n Pfand,
o Pfandrecht,
p Realkredit,
q Schuldner,
r Vertrag,
s Wechseldiskontierung,
t Zahlungsverzug,
u Zedent,
v Zession.

2 Questions on the text. You can use for your answers the definitions given in the text.

a How can a loan be secured by joint liability?
b Which requirement has to be met so that a surety can be understood as a one-sided liability agreement?
c How can a bank loan be secured by an assignment?
d What are pledges in the form of land and property used for?
e What is the difference between a land charge and a mortgage?

3 Explain in about 3 to 4 sentences how loans can be secured by means of a surety.

Say it in English: Applying for a loan

Use straightforward English in translating the following details.

1 Herr Jones, ein englischer Ingenieur, der zur Zeit in Erlangen arbeitet, beantragt einen Dispositionskredit bei unserer Bank.

2 Er muß deswegen einen Kreditantrag ausfüllen und genaue Angaben zu seiner Person und zu seinen finanziellen Verhältnissen machen.

3 Fragen Sie ihn nach folgenden Einzelheiten:

- **a** Familienname / Vorname / Geburtstag / Familienstand / unterhaltsberechtigte Kinder (mit Altersangabe)
- **b** dauernder Wohnsitz / seit wann / Eigentümer oder Mieter / genaue Anschrift mit Postleitzahl / vorherige Adresse
- **c** ausführende Tätigkeit / Stellung / wie lange
- **d** Name und Anschrift der Firma / Geschäftszweig / Sparte
- **e** vorheriger Arbeitgeber (wenn weniger als drei Jahre bei derzeitiger Firma beschäftigt)
- **f** persönliche Angaben des Ehegatten (zum Beispiel Mädchenname)
- **g** Beruf des Ehegatten
- **h** Name und Anschrift der Firma des Ehegatten
- **i** regelmäßige monatliche Bezüge / Nettoeinkommen / andere Einkommen / Einkommen des Ehegatten / Summe aller Bezüge nach Steuern
- **j** Wert des Grundstücks oder Hauses (falls Haus- oder Grundstückseigentümer) / geschätzter Wert / Belastungen?
- **k** regelmäßige monatliche Zahlungsverpflichtungen:
  - monatliche Belastung (Grundschuld / Hypothek)
  - Miete
  - Lebensversicherung
  - Ratenkredit / Anschaffungsdarlehen
  - andere regelmäßige Zahlungsverpflichtungen
  - Summe (total) aller Zahlungsverpflichtungen
- **l** Bankkonten bei anderen Kreditinstituten / Banken / Bausparkassen / Postgiroamt
- **m** Verwendung des Kredits

4 Welche Sicherheiten können Sie bieten?

5 Wir gewähren Kredite zu äußerst günstigen Konditionen.

6 Wie berechnen Sie die Raten? Woraus besteht eine Rate?

7 Eine Rate besteht aus Tilgungsbetrag, Zins und Bearbeitungsgebühren.

8 Die Kreditabteilung prüft die Kreditwürdigkeit des Antragstellers.

9 Der Kredit wird entweder in laufender Rechnung oder als Darlehen gewährt.

10 Wenn der Kredit genehmigt ist, erhalten Sie von uns ein Bewilligungsschreiben, das folgende Punkte enthält:
Art und Höhe des bewilligten Kredits, Kreditkosten, Kündigung, Sicherung und Tilgung des Kredits, Zeitpunkt der Bereitstellung, Allgemeine Geschäftsbedingungen.

11 Ich bestätige ausdrücklich die Richtigkeit vorstehender Angaben.

12 Ich / Wir stimme / n zu, daß die Bank jederzeit berechtigt ist, zum Zwecke der Kreditprüfung Auskünfte bei Dritten einzuholen oder Auszüge bzw. Abschriften anzufordern.

Unit 10
Loans for private investments

Part A

Extra money for any reason?

Use Your All-Purpose Home Secured Loan
For Any Reason You Choose.

Pay off other loans and credit accounts

Education Expenses

Home Improvements

Major Purchases

And Take Up To 10 Years To Repay!

Answer the following introductory questions.

1. What could you need extra money for?
2. Where could you go to get the money?
3. What conditions would have to be fulfilled in order for you to get the money?
4. Would there be any extra cost to you? If so, which?
5. Would it be better to overdraw your bank account or take out a loan? What information do you need to make this decision?
6. Are there any advantages of being in debt?

Common types of loans

Reasons for borrowing money
There are many reasons for borrowing money. You may want to make a major purchase such as a home, car, boat, washing-machine or some other home appliance. Or you may want to remodel your house, put in a new kitchen or install a swimming pool. Some day you may be in the position of having to finance your children's education. Then again you may simply want to consolidate a number of smaller debts. Whatever your financial needs, it pays to shop around. Both the types of loans available and the cost of borrowing money vary considerably.

Types of loans
In the U.S.A., as in Britain, loan programs can be tailored to meet an individual's special situation. Basically, loans can be divided into two categories: **secured** and **unsecured.** If you own your own home, you can use the equity built up over the years as collateral to secure a loan. In this case the bank is sure that no matter what happens it will get its money back, and therefore it is taking virtually no risk. The result is lower costs for you, the borrower. On the other hand, if you have nothing to put up as collateral, the bank is taking a greater risk and thus charges you a higher rate of interest.

Home equity loan
One of the most common types of **secured loans** is known as a home equity loan and most banks offer two types. The traditional one can be had at either a variable or a fixed interest rate. Once your application is approved, you receive a lump sum for a specific purpose and pay off interest and principal over the life of the loan. On variable interest rate loans, the rate moves in line with prevailing market rates. If you choose a fixed-rate home equity loan, your interest and monthly payments will remain constant for the duration of the loan. This allows you to budget monthly payments easily.
Home equity loans can also be a revolving line of credit, available for 10 years or more. This type of loan allows you access to your line of credit at any time. You may find it convenient to be able to borrow the amount of money you need simply by writing a cheque. You can borrow up to the maximum of your credit line. You pay interest only on the amount you actually use. Home equity loans usually involve closing costs, which can amount to 2 %–3 % of the amount of the loan and vary according to the amount being borrowed and the area in which you live. Since the maximum amount that can be borrowed depends on the market value of your home, which in turn makes it possible to determine the amount of equity you have built up, a number of services must be performed. The fees for these services make up the closing costs and include things like appraisal fee, filing fees, title insurance and mortgage recording tax. Usually, the closing costs can be deducted from the amount of the loan, i.e. you don't actually pay them in cash. As with most loans, there is also an application fee. Often this is the only "up-front" cost you must pay at the closing.

Other types
Other types of secured loans include car and boat loans. In these cases the bank accepts the car or boat as collateral, and there are no closing costs. However, the interest rate on these types of loans is usually higher than with a home equity loan. The same is true of home improvement loans. These types of loans are advisable if you don't need a large amount of money, i.e. less than $ 20,000.00.
Unsecured loans, also known as personal loans may work well when you want to consolidate debt, pay off bills, take a vacation, or at any time when you need a source of short-term credit.
Suppose, for example, that you want to combine all your credit card and department store bills into one lump and pay less interest overall. If you are paying an average interest rate of about 20 % on these, you may want to consider paying 12 to 16 percent on a typi-

cal unsecured personal loan instead. Keep in mind, however, that if you have any assets, including a savings account, which you can use as collateral, you may be able to take out a secured loan instead. This could result in a 3–4 percent lower APR than on unsecured loans.

Whenever you need money follow the same rules you would use when buying a new car. Compare offers and hidden costs, figure out whether your monthly payment will fit into your budget, and try to find the best deal available.

1 Find the appropriate explanations in Column B for the expressions in Column A.

	Column A		*Column B*
A	application fee	**a**	to combine into one
B	interest	**b**	length of time something lasts
C	major purchase	**c**	easy
D	consolidate	**d**	practically
E	vary	**e**	fluctuate, not stay the same
F	virtually	**f**	fee paid for the use of money
G	lump sum	**g**	charge for processing a request for a loan
H	principal	**h**	the amount of money lent and on which interest is paid
I	duration	**i**	an expensive item that is bought
J	convenient	**j**	an amount of money given or received as a single unit rather than in installments

2 Answer the following questions.

a Why is it important to compare loan offers?

b What is the difference between the two types of home equity loans?

c Compare the advantages and disadvantages of fixed interest and variable interest rates when borrowing money.

d When would someone take out an unsecured loan?

3 Decide which of the following statements are true and which are false.

a It doesn't make any difference what kind of loan you take out when you need money. They're all the same anyway.

b Anybody can take out a home equity loan.

c Banks prefer to grant secured loans.

d A fixed interest rate never changes.

e A car loan is usually unsecured.

f Homeowners can usually get better loan conditions than people who rent their homes.

Get the low-rate loan you want, at a payment you can afford.

Auto

- Choose the new or used car you want – any make or model, foreign or domestic.
- Make lower monthly payments with our extended terms:
  - As long as 60 months* on new cars (this year or prior year models).
  - As long as 48 months on used cars up to six years old.
- 100 % financing for loan terms up to 48 months on new or used cars – no down payment necessary.
- Take up to 60 months on a new car, with a 20 % down payment.
- Take up to 90 days after loan approval to shop around for the car of your choice.

Marine

- Finance new or used boat models up to ten years old.
- Convenient terms of up to 180 months.**
- Take up to 90 days after loan approval to shop around for the boat of your dreams.
- Refinance an existing boat loan with our favorable rates and terms.

Home Improvement

- Convenient terms from 24 to 120 months.***
- 100 % financing.
- Upon approval, take up to 30 days to shop around for the materials or contractor of your choice.

Personal

- For vacations, education or medical expenses, furniture – whatever you choose.
- Convenient terms of 24 to 60 months.
- Take up to 30 days after loan approval to shop for the best deal, or to finalize your plans.

Q. What's the advantage of an installment loan over other forms of credit?

A. An installment loan is a smart way to use credit. It can be a more affordable alternative to credit cards or a line of credit when making a large purchase. In fact, you can often reduce your expenses by paying off your high-cost credit balances with a low-rate installment loan.

Q. How can an installment loan make my life easier?

A. Unlike charge cards or lines of credit, an installment loan lets you make fixed payments for a predetermined length of time. So payments are predictable – and more manageable – and you're in better control of your budget.

Q. Is there a penalty if I pay back the amount I owe all at once?

A. No. You can pay your outstanding balance at any time without incurring a prepayment penalty.

Q. When is my first monthly payment due?

A. Within thirty to forty-five days after you receive your check.

* Borrowing $ 8,000 at 10 50 % APR for 60 months will result in monthly payments of approximately $ 171 96

** Borrowing $ 25,000 at 10 60 % APR for 180 months will result in monthly payments of approximately $ 277 98

*** Borrowing $ 7,000 at 12 50 % APR for 120 months will result in monthly payments of approximately $ 102 48

Rates and terms are subject to change. All loans are subject to credit approval.

(Chemical Bank)

1 You want to get a loan for buying a used car. What are the terms offered?

2 What is the annual percentage rate (APR) offered for a home improvement loan with an extended term of 120 months?

3 Why can installment loans be a more affordable alternative to credit cards?

Dialogue: Home improvement loan

Part D

A customer comes to a bank to find out about the various types of financing open to him. He wants to put an extension on his house, which is about 40 years old and which he has owned for the last ten years. He intends to do most of the work himself and expects it to cost about $ 15,000.00.

Write a dialogue between the homeowner and the bank clerk, making sure that both parties find out all the pertinent information. You may supply any information you think appropriate.

Balance sheet evaluation

Part E

Balance sheet evaluation has the task of discovering, with the help of the reference figures obtained of the analysis of the balance sheet, information regarding the financial situation, the efficiency and the growth prospects of the enterprise or business.
The profit analysis provides an overview of the expenditure and revenue structure of the enterprise.

Study the following "Five Year Comparative Statement" of a British business firm and discuss
- the development of profits,
- the structure of fixed assets,
- the relationships between share capital, reserves and liabilities.

Five Year Comparative Statement

Revenue account	£'000s	£'000s	£'000s	£'000s	£'000s
Turnover	82 219	87 837	96 122	101 331	117 296
Depreciation	1 580	1 921	2 126	2 397	2 896
Other Expenses	19 118	20 403	22 696	23 940	26 072
Trading Surplus	1 744	1 885	1 786	1 185	1 817
Dividend Stamps and other Benefits	836	868	955	993	962
Property Income – Operating Leases	191	249	272	320	317
Interest and Dividends Receivable	248	290	132	45	41
Retained Surplus	483	387	1 575	1 509	2 040

Balance sheet

Fixed Assets					
Intangible Assets	130	101	94	75	41
Tangible Assets – owned	10 517	11 984	16 150	21 713	22 532
Tangible Assets – leased		249	273	1 045	868
Investments	487	439	440	440	441
Current Assets					
Stocks	5 726	6 947	7 272	7 776	8 662
Debtors and Prepayments	4 339	4 919	3 095	2 963	3 375
Investments	1 802	1 264	182	143	134
Cash	280	247	261	266	284
Current Liabilities					
Creditors	8 330	10 225	9 950	10 130	11 689
Loans	580	590	680	693	597
Long Term Liabilities					
Creditors	661	741	839	948	1 091
Loans		218	239	5 040	3 505
Provision for Deferred Taxation	356	548	575	542	303
Net Assets	**13 354**	**13 828**	**15 484**	**17 068**	**19 152**
Share Capital	4 309	4 398	4 472	4 548	4 592
Reserves	9 032	9 413	10 992	12 499	14 539
Minority Holdings	13	17	20	21	21
Ratio of Dividend Stamps to Trading Surplus	% 47.94	% 46.05	% 53.47	% 83.80	% 52.94

(Adapted from: Plymouth + South Devon Co-operative Society)

Unit 11
Types of securities

Stock market terminology – easy to understand?

Part A

Investing in the stock market

When people first consider investing in the stock market they often need to master a whole new language.

> "Are you interested in *equities, options* or *financial futures?*"
> "Do you want to purchase *common* or *preferred shares?*"
> "Would you like *voting* or *non-voting stock?*"
> "Would you prefer *issues* that are *convertible, redeemable, retractable callable* or *participating?*"

But the language is not difficult to learn. Market terminology is easy when you know how the market works.

These definitions will help you for the beginning:

Cumulative dividend
All unpaid dividends accumulate in arrears. They must be paid before common dividends are paid.

Callable (or redeemable) shares
The company reserves the right to redeem the shares for cancellation.

Retractable shares
The holder of retractable shares may hand them in to the company on a specific date at a fixed price.

Convertible shares
These shares may be converted into some other class of stock at a pre-determined price.

Voting shares
Owners of common shares possess the right of taking part in decisions in the Annual General Meeting of the company.

Variable or floating rate shares
Variable preferred shares pay dividend amounts that fluctuate to reflect changes in interest rates.

Participating shares
The holders of these shares have certain rights to the earnings of a company over their specified dividend rate.

Blue chip stocks
They are usually common shares of well-established companies with a long record of good earnings and dividend payments.

Growth stocks
Common stock of a company with excellent prospects for above average future growth.

Penny stocks
Low-priced, often speculative issues, selling at less than $1.00 a share.

Listed stock
A stock of a company which is traded on a stock exchange.

Unlisted stock
A stock not listed which is traded on the Over-the-Counter market.

1 Did you understand the definitions?

a What is the advantage of a cumulative dividend?
b What is the disadvantage for a shareholder if shares are cancelled?
c What can a shareholder do with retractable shares?
d Describe a situation in which it can be good for you to possess convertible shares.
e How can you use a voting right?
f Why are there floating rates?
g What is the advantage for owners of participating shares?
h What are the pros and cons of growth stocks and blue chip stocks?
i Why are penny stocks a risky investment?
j Is a stock exchange needed for the Over-the-Counter market?

2 Find German translations for the technical terms.

3 Match the following business terms with the appropriate definitions given below and try to find a German translation.

Business terms:

equities/option/futures/common shares/preferred shares

Definitions:

a contracts to buy or sell specific quantities of a commodity or financial instrument with delivery delayed until some agreed upon time in the next years
b securities issued by a company which represent part ownership in the company
c contracts which give the holder the right to buy or sell a fixed amount of a certain stock at a specific price within a specific time
d common and preferred shares issued by a company which represent ownership to the company
e shares issued by a company to raise additional capital with dividends which must be paid before any dividends are paid to common shareholders

Part B — How much profit do you get from your securities?

A reporter (R.) interviews Bruce McLaren (B. M.), financial expert.

R. More and more readers of our magazine intend to buy securities. They are no longer content with the returns they get for money in a savings account.

B. M. I can understand that a great part of the well-informed readers of your magazine try to get a higher yield for their money. Buying securities is the right decision in the present situation. But people should not forget that there is a price risk in the securities' business especially if one's portfolio consists mainly of shares.

R. Does that mean that you would recommend to buy fixed-interest securities instead of shares?

B. M. As I've already pointed out a portfolio should consist of both shares and bonds. Bonds are issued by various institutions, e.g. the Government or private corporations, in order to raise medium- or long-term funds. When you buy one of these you are granted a fixed interest-rate which is paid to you until maturity. There is no risk of losing your money because it is backed by the assets of the issuer and by mortgages.

R. That sounds really great. But what are the disadvantages?

B. M. As you are only lending money, you won't have a say in the enterprise. Furthermore, depending on the level of interest-rates during the term, the company can repay the money prematurely. With shares you are among the owners of the company. That means you have the privilege of participation in the company's annual general meeting.

R. Participation is an important aspect. But most people are more interested in the price of shares and in the returns they can earn.

B. M. I'll deal with your point concerning returns first. A stock corporation produces profits and shareholders are entitled to a dividend. How much they get depends on the performance of the company. Referring to your second point I'd like to remind your readers that the prices of shares are fixed at the stock exchange and are not only influenced by the growth of the individual company but also by political events and speculative movements. Finally we must not forget that the customer has to pay for brokerage and commission.

R. You must have a good knowledge of the securities' market in order to consider all these aspects. Isn't it much easier to buy investment trusts as an alternative to shares and bonds?

B. M. Investment certificates are issued by mutual funds and represent equal shares in the portfolio. There are different kinds of funds, e.g. bond or equity funds. The mixed portfolio funds try to utilise the benefits of bonds and stocks alike.

R. Are there any other financial instruments to be had on the market?

B. M. Yes, of course. You remember what I said about fixed-interest securities? Some companies issue bonds which can be converted into stocks after a certain period. You have to analyse the market and the specific company to decide whether a conversion really suits your financial needs.

R. Summing up all the information given so far, I think a mixed portfolio would possibly meet our readers' interests best.

B. M. That's absolutely right. But even with a mixed portfolio you must have a good knowledge of the securities' market. The best advice I can give to the non-expert readers is to rely on the investment advisers of their bank.

1 Answer the following questions on the text.

- **a** Why are savings accounts no longer very popular?
- **b** What types of securities should a portfolio consist of?
- **c** Why are fixed-interest securities without risk for the buyer?
- **d** Explain "to repay prematurely".
- **e** How can a shareholder take part in the decision-taking process of a firm?
- **f** Which factors influence prices and dividends of shares?
- **g** Are there any expenses a buyer of shares has to pay?

2 Make up a table in your notebook following the layout given here and fill in what you know about the following aspects of the different types of securities:
issuer; return; risk; cost; advantages and disadvantages.

Aspect	Stocks	Fixed-interest securities	Investment certificates
issuer	company	government or private corporation	investment trust
return	—	—	—
risk	—	—	—
cost	—	—	—
advantages	—	—	—
disadvantages	—	—	—

3 Find out which of these statements are true. Make the false statements correct.

a Fixed-interest securities are short-term financial instruments.
b Fixed-interest securities may only be purchased by individuals.
c Stocks are redeemed at a predetermined date.
d Governments often issue fixed-interest securities.
e A small shareholder can influence the price of stocks.
f The Annual General Meeting is a forum to inform the company's employees about future projects.
g Shares are backed by the performance and the total assets of the company.
h Each type of securities consists of a certificate and the coupons.

4 Find synonyms and antonyms. Write the missing words in your note-book.

Synonyms	Antonyms
to acquire – to buy – to p— to advise – to r— clerk – e— interest – y—, r— face value – n— value	short term – l— term fixed interest – v— interest equity – d— to raise money – to s— money to debit one's account – to c— to place (an order) – to c—

Part C

What causes stock prices to rise and fall?

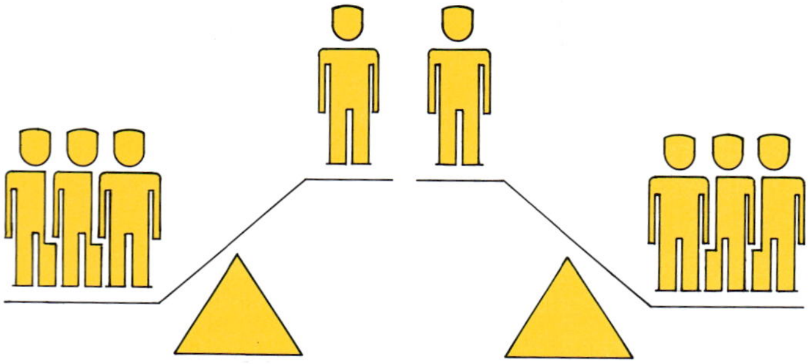

Stock prices are determined by supply and demand in the market place. If there are more orders to buy a given issue than offers to sell, prices will rise. If the offers to sell exceed the orders to buy, prices will fall. The price of a stock will then reflect investors' overall opinion of the prospects of that company's shares. This opinion will be influenced by many factors, including:

- company's earnings, dividend record and outlook
- company's growth prospects
- type of industry or service
- individual and corporate taxes
- capital market conditions (ie. inflation, interest rates, etc.)

Newspaper Listing

1 Highest and lowest price paid for the stock to date this year. This stock has traded as high as $17.00, and as low as $14-3/4 during the year. Shares traded under $5.00 are quoted in cents.

2 Abbreviated name of the company issuing the stock.

Year High	Year Low	Stock	Div.	High	Low	Close	Change	Vol.
S 17	S14-3/4	Acme T. & D.	S. 72	S16-3/4	S16-1/8	S16-1/8	-5/8	[illegible]00
29-3/8	26	Comput Co.	2.28	29-1/4	29-1/4	29-1/4	[illegible]/8	100
15	7-7/8	O & G Expl. A		9	8-3/4	8-7/8	-1/8	14400
8	490	Ven. Mining		5-1/2	5-1/2	5-1/2	-1/8 z	20
3/4	26-1/2	Sec. Bank	2.00	27	26-1/2	27	+1/4	19626
345	280	Alpha Oil		280	270	280	-5	30500
15-1/4	13-1/2	Imp Trus	1.20	13-1/2	[illegible]2-1/4	13-1/4	-1/8	64353
11-1/2	7-3/4	Gamma Res		9-5/8	[illegible]-1/8	9-3/8	-1/8	9724

3 Annual dividend paid by the company. This is a projected annual rate based on dividend payments over the last twelve months.

4 Highest price paid for the stock during this trading session was $5-1/2, and the lowest was $5-1/2 as well.

5 Price paid for the last board lot traded was $8-7/8. This was down 1/8 or 12.5 cents from the closing price in the previous session.

6 Number of shares traded during the trading session. The symbol z indicates that less than a board lot traded.

(Adapted from: Market Makers, The Toronto Stock Exchange)

1 Look at the table below and form sentences according to the following examples:

- *With 43 offered and 37 ordered shares supply exceeds demand and so prices will fall.*
- *With a demand for 37 shares compared to a supply of 43 prices will fall.*

Stock	Offers	Orders	Prices
Acme T&D	43	37	fall
Comput Co.	230	277	rise
SecBank	91	93	rise
Alpha Oil	2 347	2 185	fall
Imp Trust	841	806	fall

2 Which three factors are, in your opinion, most important for investors' decisions to buy shares of a company?
Compare your list with that of your neighbour and discuss the reasons for your choice.

3 What is the meaning of these terms occurring in the newspaper listing?

- **a** stock (number 1)
- **b** abbreviated (no. 2)
- **c** projected (no. 3)
- **d** trading session (no. 4)
- **e** board lot (nos. 5 and 6)
- **f** closing price (no. 5)

Part D

Going global – to the 1890s?

Investors in government bonds no longer need to be told that they are part of a global market: they happily trade bonds in dollars, German marks or yen, and take for granted the link between the yields on these assets and the ups and downs of currencies. What goes for bonds, it seems, should also apply to equities.

The first signs of this shift towards a truly global equity market explain some of the things which local market-watchers have found odd. One such oddity is the overvaluation of Wall Street. The yield on American Treasury bonds is currently 9 %. To provide a similar return, a representative basket of American shares would need a price-earnings ratio of around 11. But the average p/e ratio of the Standard and Poor's index of 400 industrial companies is 24.

Measures of value should take account of foreign share prices. Wall Street's p/e ratio has long been lower than Tokyo's. America's p/e is also much lower than Singapore's. In the eyes of their investors, American equities ought to look bargain-priced.

The hard question is how far the different countries' p/e ratios will converge as the global equity market develops. They will never be neatly equal. As long as exchange rates float up and down, prices will have to take account of currency risk. Differences in the taxation of income from equities, in accounting, in the regulation of markets, and in what might loosely be called the investment culture will also cause the ratios to diverge.

In some ways, America's financial markets have an 1880s look about them. A hundred

years ago America depended, as it does now, on imported foreign capital, most of which arrived through sales of shares and bonds rather than through bank lending.
The bear markets of the late nineteenth century all therefore sprang from interruptions in the flow of foreign money. In 1893 and again in 1896, the cash stopped because of fears that America would abandon the gold standard and devalue the dollar. Financial markets really have seen it all before.

(Adapted from: The Economist)

1 Read the short definitions and find German translations.

a	*bond*	a written promise to pay a sum of money
b	*global*	concerning the whole world
c	*to take for granted*	to accept
d	*link*	connection
e	*yield*	what you get for an investment
f	*assets*	the portfolio of an investor
g	*currency*	money used in a country
h	*equity*	ordinary shares
i	*odd*	unusual
j	*return*	profit
k	*bargain*	goods bought at a favourable price
l	*to converge*	to come together
m	*exchange rate*	two currencies compared with each other
n	*accounting*	to do the financial records of a firm
o	*to diverge*	to go into different directions
p	*bear market*	expecting a fall in prices
q	*to abandon*	to leave for ever
r	*to devalue*	to reduce the foreign value of money

2 Answer the following questions on the text.

a What is the special risk of trading bonds in different countries?
b How much is the average p/e ratio of American shares?
c What evidence indicates that there is an overvaluation at Wall Street?
d Why do American shares look bargain-priced?
e Why will the different countries' p/e ratios never be equal? (5 reasons)
f How are America's financial markets similar to those of 1890? How are they different from 1890?
g Could there be a bear market in the late 20th century
– according to the text,
– according to your opinion?

3 What do you know about these expressions and facts?

a Wall Street
b American Treasury bonds
c a representative basket of shares
d price-to-earnings ratio
e Standard and Poor's index
f bear market
g gold standard

Part E

Interview on securities trade in Germany

A representative from Lloyds Bank in London is spending some days at your bank and wants to get some information. Write down complete answers covering all aspects of the questions of your colleague from Britain.

a I've heard that in Germany banks are dealers in securities. Is that a profitable business? What do they charge?

b What is the current rate of interest for government bonds? How secure are these bonds and in which denominations can they be had?

c Is there a tax on the earnings of a share? What is the average percentage of the dividend offered by German PLCs?

d Can you give me some examples of growth stocks on the one hand and blue chip stocks on the other hand? Are there also convertible shares in Germany?

e Last week I read in a newspaper article that Tokyo's p/e ratio is the highest in the Western industrialised countries. What about the price of German shares compared to the profit you can get from this investment?

f I was told that German investors don't like to bet like we English do. Therefore they are said to be very careful as to speculative securities and prefer buying investments funds. Is there a strong demand for investment certificates among your customers?

Unit 12
Stock Exchanges in Britain and America

Part A

What is the history of the British Stock Exchange?

Dealings in stocks and shares began in the 17th Century. Gradually an informal market developed around the coffee houses in the City of London. In 1773 "New Jonathan's" Coffee House became the Stock Exchange. The growth of the Industrial Revolution prompted the establishment of more than 30 local share markets in other parts of the country. By 1967 the "Country" Exchanges had grouped themselves into six Regional Exchanges, and in 1973 all seven Exchanges in the British Isles amalgamated to form the Stock Exchange of Great Britain and Ireland. Now the Stock Exchange is undergoing the greatest and most rapid period of change in its history. "Big Bang" is a phrase coined to describe the 27th October 1986. On this day the Exchange abolished the system of minimum commissions and introduced new electronic dealing systems.

Handicap

1. How did the London Stock Exchange develop?
2. Where are the stock exchanges in Germany?
3. Why is it a handicap to have so many stock exchanges in Germany?
4. How did "Big Bang" change the London Stock Exchange?
5. Is there anything similar to "Big Bang" in the German stock exchange system?

Part B Problems of the London Stock Exchange

Unlike its counterparts in the USA or Japan, the British system has traditionally been based on a division not only between banks, which are restricted from underwriting shares on the market, and investment and securities houses, which are able to deal in stocks on the market, but also between brokers and jobbers.

A client wanting to buy or sell stocks would go first to a broker who, acting on his commission, would then go down to the floor and tour the jobbers holding that stock. He would ask each the selling and buying price without revealing which interested him particularly. Having found the best price, he would arrange the transaction.

Similarly, a corporation wanting to raise money on the Stock Exchange or to buy shares in a potential take-over candidate would normally go first to a merchant bank, which would use a broker to do the buying or launch the issue.

The separation of functions was based not simply on tradition but also on a profound belief that such a separation was the only safe way of protecting the interests of the client. With a broker acting solely in the interests of the client and working on a straight fee or commission, and the jobber gaining his percentage on the actual dealing, there was no temptation for the broker to persuade his clients to buy shares that he was holding on his own account or to sell shares that he was short of.

To survive, however, such a system needs minimum guaranteed commissions if most of the brokers are not to be forced out of business in a scramble for business through commission-cutting. The independent broker's only alternative to set commissions is either to become a low-cost, high-volume discount broker or to hope that the client is prepared to pay him voluntarily a high commission for his research and advice, which is unlikely. If he cannot do either he has to seek to diversify, joining a bigger bank grouping in which he becomes part of the client service. The trouble with the merger route is that you lose your independence and probably a good deal of attraction to your client as well. Whether the Stock Exchange understood that removing the brick of set commissions would make the whole house unsteady is not clear.

(Adapted from: Adrian Hamilton, The Financial Revolution, Harmondsworth)

1 What is the meaning of "would" in the second paragraph?

2 Answer the following questions on the text.

- **a** How have the roles of banks and investment and securities houses traditionally been divided in Britain?
- **b** Who were the dealers and agents in the traditional stock exchange?
- **c** How did the brokers find the best price?
- **d** What was the procedure if a business firm needed money?
- **e** Why was the separation of functions good for the client?
- **f** What could a broker do if there was no guaranteed commission?
- **g** What can brokers do now that minimum commissions have been abolished?

3 What do you think about these effects of the "Big Bang"?

- **a** New firms can become corporate members of the London Stock Exchange.
- **b** A firm of brokers/dealers has the option of becoming a committed market maker. (To become a market maker means to combine the functions of a broker and a jobber in one firm.)
- **c** Commissions are negotiable between brokers and their clients.

Why is the New York Stock Exchange so important?

The New York Stock Exchange is three times the size of Tokyo's and eight times as large as London's. A roll call of the new instruments of today's world capital markets – variable-rate and convertible bonds, bonds with warrants and deep-discount bonds, financial options and futures, securitized mortgage and automobile-leasing pools – is a catalogue of innovations by American banks in American markets. Any major international company considering launching itself on the global stock market thinks of issuing simultaneous share offerings in New York as well as its home market. When Reuters went public, shares were on sale in New York at the same time as in London. When the British government wished to offer public shares in the state utility British Telecom, it did so in New York – through American investment houses as well as in London. In being able to handle huge issues without a hiccup, the New York Stock Exchange has shown what 'liquidity' means.

The British decision to end fixed commissions in the London Stock Exchange comes a full ten years after Wall Street ended fixed commissions on what was to become known as 'May Day', 1 May 1975.

(Adapted from: Hamilton, s.a.)

Trading around the clock: Central European Time

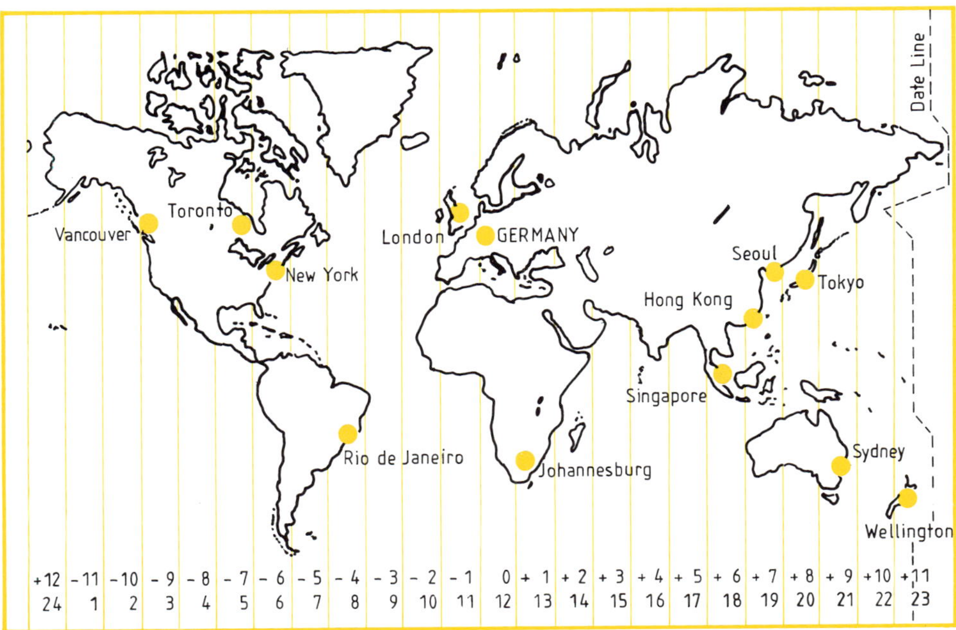

(Adapted from: Federation of the German Stock Exchanges, Annual Report)

1 Answer the following questions on the text.

a Where do the new instruments of the world capital markets come from?
b Who do many international companies prefer the New York Stock Exchange for the issue of shares?
c Explain the term 'liquidity' (line 22).
d What is meant by the expression 'without a hiccup' (line 21)?
e What happened on 'May Day' 1975 (line 28)?

2 Find German translations for the following technical terms.

a variable-rate bond (line 4)
b convertible bond (line 5)
c bonds with warrants (line 5)
d deep-discount bonds (line 6)
e financial options and futures (line 6)
f securitized mortgage (line 7)
g automobile-leasing pools (line 8)
h public shares (line 17)
i state utility (line 18)

3 What is the meaning of the following words with -ing forms?

a considering (line 11)
b launching (line 11)
c issuing (line 12)
d in being able (line 20)

4 What do you know about these names?

a Reuters (line 14)
b British Telecom (line 18)
c Wall Street (line 26)

Part D

A new system: NASDAQ securities dealing

NASDAQ was developed by the National Association of Securities Dealers in 1971. The system consisted of 20,000 miles of leased telephone lines connecting terminals in every dealer's office and tied into a central computing system that recorded prices, deals and other information. The dealer screens provided three levels of information. The simplest level displayed the average prices for all the stocks on the OTC – that is, the median between the bids and offer prices keyed in by members willing to make a market in a stock. The next level allowed the dealers to see the actual bid and to offer quotes themselves. The top level allowed the market-makers to put in prices for display around the computer market.

The dealer who was willing to make a market – that is, to quote a price at which he was willing to buy and a price at which he was willing to sell a particular stock – had only to key in his prices, give an indication of the volumes in which he was prepared to deal and then change the prices as demand moved the market and his own position. All the buyer or seller had to do was to look at the screen for the range of bids and offers being quoted by various dealers and then call one or more when he wanted to make a deal.

Within the next dozen years the share volume rose by more than sixteen times, and the number of terminals in use rose from barely a few thousand in 1972 to 40,000 in 1978 and more than 120,000 in 1985. By then the volume of share dealing made NASDAQ the third largest stock exchange in the world, smaller only than those of New York and Tokyo and greater than those of London, Zurich, Germany, Toronto and Paris put together. And all of this through the medium of telephone lines.

(Adapted from: Hamilton, s.a.)

1 Here are several possible definitions for some words from the text. Which of them is correct according to the context?

a deal (line 6, 29): (1) an agreement or arrangement
(2) a large or considerable quantity
(3) a particular type of treatment that is given or received
(4) the process of giving out cards to players

b bid (line 11, 14): (1) an offer to pay a certain price at a sale
(2) an offer to do some work at a certain price
(3) an attempt to get, win or attract something

c quote (line 14): (1) a phrase taken from a work of literature
(2) the calculated cost of a piece of work
(3) statement of the current price of an article

2 Find the correct form of the words given.
Words: to deal in, to deal with, to quote, to offer

a The company's shares are currently ___ at 90 pence.
b All complaints will be ___ by the manager.
c A shop ___ goods of all sorts.
d They've ___ us $60,000.00 for the house.

3 Find the words from the text corresponding to these translations into German.

a speichern (line 6)
b Nachfrage (line 11)
c Informationsstufe (line 13)
d Händler (line 13)
e ein Angebot machen (line 14)
f Handel treiben (line 18)
g Bandbreite (line 27)
h Wertpapierhandel (line 35)

Speech: Stock Exchanges in Germany

Part E

Prepare a speech containing all the information given below. Your speech should not be a word-by-word translation but include all the important facts.
There is a group of junior bank trainees from Portugal visiting your bank. All of them can speak English. You are told to inform them about how the German stock exchanges work. The head of your department provides you with the following information:

a In Deutschland entstand die erste Börse zu Beginn des 16. Jahrhunderts. Heute gibt es in Deutschland 8 Wertpapierbörsen.

b Zutritt in den Börsensaal haben Kursmakler, Bankenvertreter und Presseleute. Zuschauer sind gerne gesehen. Der Kursmakler stellt den Börsenpreis fest. Er ist Einzelkaufmann.

c Die Geschäfte an der Börse werden zwischen Kursmakler und Wertpapierhändler abgeschlossen. Die Wertpapierhändler sind die Vertreter der Banken im Börsensaal.

d Nach Feststellung des Kurses wird ein Schlußschein ausgestellt, auf dem Käufer und Verkäufer, der Ausführungskurs sowie die Courtage angegeben sind.

e Für ihre Bemühungen erhält die Bank eine Provision, die im allgemeinen bei Renten 0,5 % vom Nominalbetrag und bei Aktien 1 % vom Kurswert beträgt. In den meisten Fällen hat der Anleger eine Maklergebühr zu entrichten.

f Voraussetzung für den Handel der Wertpapiere an der Börse ist die Zulassung. Die Zulassung bedeutet, daß Wertpapier und Aussteller sich gewissen Formalitäten unterzogen haben. Kern des Zulassungsverfahrens ist ein umfangreicher Prospekt über Wertpapier und Emittent, der vor der Einführung des Wertpapiers zum Handel und zur amtlichen Notierung in der Presse veröffentlicht und auch gesondert gedruckt wird.

Unit 13
Investment funds offer more security

Part A What investment experts can do for you

Why is it safer to invest your money in co-operation with investment experts?

Without experts it is up to you to do the following before investing money in shares:

- You can read newspapers (national and international) to get information about the stock market.
- You can find out price tendencies of securities by making your own lists of price developments or by using a computer program.
- You can use personal contacts with businessmen (if you have any) to find out important news about the future development of companies and their share prices.

Now be honest:

1 Have you got enough time and the capacity to do all this?
2 Wouldn't it be better for you to consult an investment expert?
3 What is the real advantage of getting an investment expert's advice?

If you invest in Unit Trusts, all decisions are taken for you by investment experts who are in constant touch with world stock markets and are in possession of much more detailed information to enable decisions to be taken on a daily basis.

The highly experienced team of portfolio managers covers all the major investment markets of the world with supporting analytical research staff and ready access to research material from a wide range of external sources. Of course, no one can forecast future market trends with complete accuracy, and it must be remembered that the price of units, and the income from them, can go down as well as up. You should therefore be prepared to hold a Unit Trust investment for a period of at least two years.

(Adapted from a leaflet by TSB)

The advantages of unit trusts

When you invest in a unit trust your money is pooled in a central fund with the money of everyone else who invests in that trust and is used by the managers to invest in stocks and shares. In return, you receive units in the trust. At any time the price of your units represents a fraction of the value of every shareholding held in the trust fund.

Unlike the private investor, who may hold shares in just a few companies, a unit trust invests across a wide spectrum in different companies, sectors of the market, currencies and countries. This helps to spread risk; but if companies are successful, their shares, and the income from them, will tend to rise in value over the years.

The investments of each unit trust are looked after by professional investment managers who continuously monitor the fund's holdings and buy and sell shares according to changing market conditions.

A unit trust investor does not have to worry about taking decisions and avoids the inevitable administration which direct share ownership involves.

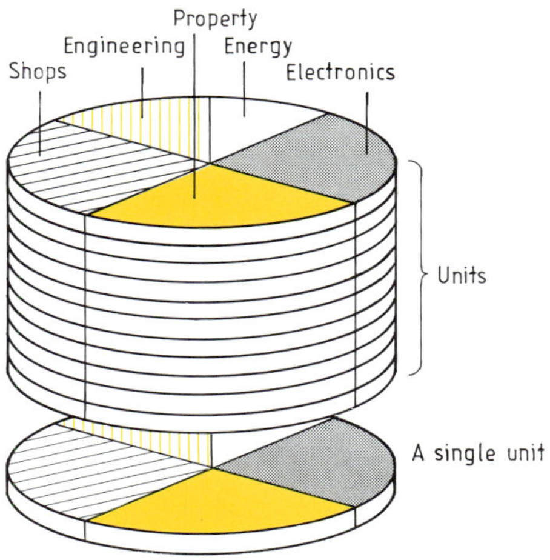

Once the trust's portfolio has been decided on, it is sub-divided into units which are then offered for sale to the public.

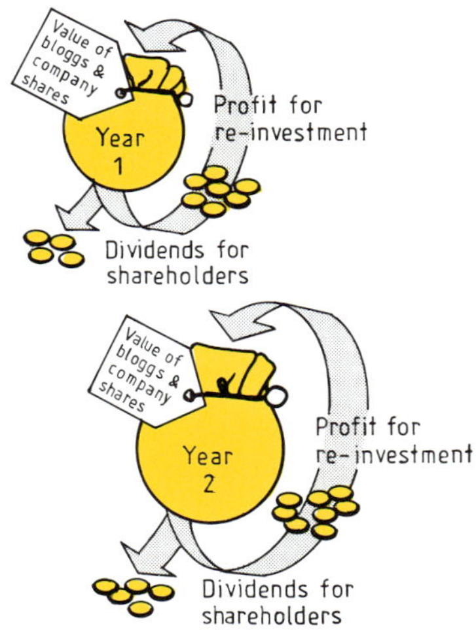

As time goes by, the money you invest in a company's shares not only grows in value, but pays you an income as well.

1. Make a definition for the term 'unit trust'.
2. Which of the following headlines fit the four paragraphs of the text?
   a Spread of Risk, **b** Capital Growth, **c** Administration, **d** Maximum Flexibility, **e** Simplicity, **f** Professional Management.
3. Unit trusts engage in a wide range of investments. Name the different investment possibilities and give examples (not in the text) for each of them.
4. What is the professional task of investment managers?
5. Why do you save time by investing money in a unit trust instead of buying shares?

Popularity and types of investment funds

Investment funds have done an enormous amount to bring new investors into the financial markets. In sheer quantity, the funds outnumber the companies listed on the Tokyo and New York stock exchanges combined. What accounts for this popularity?

For one thing the performance of investment funds has been very good – and very well advertised. But performance is hardly the only reason for the explosion in fund popularity. In an era when markets shed a quarter of their value in a single afternoon, few people can afford the time to manage actively their own investments. For individuals with $300,000.00 or more to invest, finding professional portfolio management through an investment bank, brokerage house or other financial institution is no problem.

For investors whose holdings are too small to command such personalized attention, mutual funds and other investment funds that pool investor capital can open the door to the twin benefits of professional money management and portfolio diversification.

The investment fund can also be more economical than direct investment in terms of administrative and dealing costs – and shares can even be purchased in small increments.

There is a broad spectrum of investment funds and objectives, including:

- **Balanced Funds:** invest in a mix of stocks and bonds with the objective of preserving capital while yielding current income;
- **Income Funds:** invest in high-dividend stocks and high-interest bonds to generate maximum current income;
- **Global Funds:** invest in companies traded on overseas equities markets and domestic companies with a high proportion of foreign sales;
- **Socially Conscious Funds:** select their investments according to various ethical considerations;
- **Sector and Specialized Funds:** concentrate on a single industry, country or region and as a result, can be highly volatile.

(Adapted from: Newsweek)

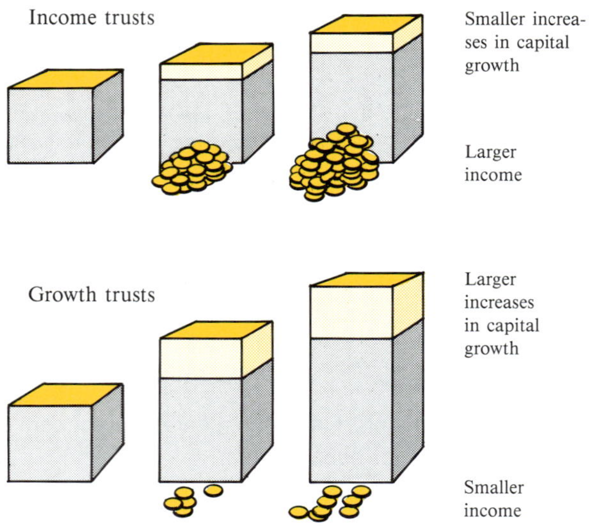

Income trusts are ideal for people looking for a healthy income and just a little capital growth. If you want to see a larger increase in your capital, with a relatively smaller income, growth trusts are a better bet.

1 Find adequate German translations. You get the meaning of the words from the short definitions.

a *to outnumber (line 3)*	to exceed in quantity
b *performance (line 7)*	something that was done well
c *to shed (line 11)*	to lose
d *mutual fund (line 20)*	American English for unit trust
e *diversification (line 24)*	a planned increase of a company's range of products
f *administrative costs (line 27)*	costs for the management of goods, money etc.
g *dealing costs (line 27)*	costs for buying and selling
h *increments (line 28)*	increase; here, quantities

2 Answer the following questions on the text.

a What evidence suggests that investment funds are very popular?

b Why are investment funds very good for investors with a small portfolio? (two reasons)

c Some individuals and companies invest huge amounts of money in shares. How can they organize the management of their portfolio?

3 Find adequate German translations for the types of funds mentioned in the text.

Buying certificates

Ms Sarah Candlin (S. C.) works as a sales representative for a British computer software firm in Germany. She has read an article about mutual funds and would like to know more about this possibility to invest money.
So she phones her bank in Germany.

Bank Clerk: Hypothekenbank. Büchner. Guten Morgen!

S. C. Guten Morgen, Herr Büchner. Ich brauche einen Rat. Darf ich bitte auf Englisch sprechen?

B. Sure, you may. What can I do for you?

S. C. My name is Sarah Candlin. I read in a newspaper article yesterday that mutual funds are a good capital investment. Does your bank offer such funds?

B. Oh yes, we really do. Buying investment certificates is very popular now. But I am not an expert as to this type of investment. I think the best would be if you came to our head office and talked with one of our real investment experts.

S. C. That's a good idea. Is it possible to make an appointment for me tomorrow afternoon?

B. Yes. I think that will be no problem. I'm booking you for tomorrow afternoon two o'clock.

S. C. Oh yes, please. 2 p.m. tomorrow.

B. But please let me have your phone number in case something unforeseeable should happen so that we can inform you about any changes in time.

S. C. Yes please. My work number is 47 89 06.

B. It is 478906. Fine. See you tomorrow, Ms Candlin.

S. C. Thank you very much for your help. Good bye.

In the afternoon of the next day Sarah Candlin arrives at the head office of the bank. She meets Dirk Lorenz (D. L.), who is one of the bank's financial experts.

This is part of their conversation:

S. C. I read an article about the popularity of mutual funds and now I'd like to talk things over with you. Which type of fund would you recommend for me?

D. L. It is difficult to say and depends primarily on your goals and the amount of money you'd like to put in. This bank favours Bigfund because it concentrates on high yield companies. There is one more advantage. There is no charge for issuing this certificate. While you are the owner all administrative work related to the certificate is also undertaken by us without any costs for you. Please take into consideration that the return varies over the years due to fluctuations of the assets in this portfolio. Furthermore you should know that – under German tax regulations – you are obliged to report those returns when you hand in your income tax declaration.

S. C. When do I get my money back?

D. L. The law governing trust companies states that they have to take back the certificates of their investors whenever the client asks for it. Please be aware of the fact that the trust company is allowed to deduct a handling fee from the net asset value.

S. C. May I take the certificates home?

D. L. Most certainly yes, but we advise against your doing so because you would fail to take advantage of our free servicing and run the risk of presenting a coupon too late.

S. C. What's the price of a single certificate?

D. L. It depends on the value of the fund's assets and the number of certificates in circulation. The one I have in mind for you is ...

1 Answer the following questions.

- **a** Which type of investment fund is Bigfund?
- **b** Why are funds – no matter which type – especially interesting for people with fairly small capital?
- **c** Why is the price per certificate rather low?
- **d** Is there a fixed or regular return for certificates?
- **e** What is the 'net asset value' of a certificate?
- **f** Why does the bank offer free servicing for certificates?

2 Write a dialogue between a bank clerk and a customer based on the following situation.

A customer wants to invest in a socially conscious fund. His capital on hand is about $50,000.00. He wants to avoid any servicing costs. You can offer a fund called "Cleanfund".

Name shares of any companies that might be included in the fund. Tell your customer that there is a good chance that the price of these certificates will go up. But he has to invest for a longer period. Your customer would like to take a certificate home (Why?). Tell him that this is possible but inform him about the disadvantages, too.

Document: The share exchange scheme

How the share exchange scheme operates

You may exchange any saleable individual shareholding worth £500 or more for Midland Bank Unit Trusts.

On the same day as we receive your share certificate and your written instructions your holding will be sold on the Stock Exchange at the current market bid price.

On the next business day the net proceeds of sale will be allocated to units in the Trust or Trusts you select at the current offer price less a discount of 2 %.

If any individual shareholding is worth £1,000 or more and is suitable for inclusion in one of the Midland Bank Unit Trust portfolios, all sale expenses may be avoided. The manager will advise on eligibility. The value of units allocated will be equal to the full offer price of your shares quoted on the Stock Exchange. In this case no contract note will be issued for your shares but you will be provided with a valuation.

You will be requested to sign a share transfer form and to surrender any dividends and allotment letters for scrip and rights issues which you may receive after the exchange, where these are due to the new owner.

If you are in any doubt about this offer you should consult your bank manager, stockbroker, solicitor, or other professional adviser.

Examples

The following examples show how the exchange of shares for units can be made advantageously:

If you sell your shares

1 000 Ordinary Shares at 100p (bid price)	£1 000.00
Less brokerage and expenses	19.27
Amount available for investment in Midland Bank Unit Trusts	£980.73
Number of units bought at say 50p each	1 961.46 units

If we sell your shares

1 000 Ordinary Shares at 100p (bid price)	£1 000.00
Less brokerage and expenses	19.27
Amount available for investment in Midland Bank Unit Trusts	£980.73
Number of units bought at say 49p each (allowing for a 2 % discount on offer price)	2 001.48 units

If we take your shares into our portfolios

1 000 Ordinary Shares at 105p (offer price)	£1 050.00
Amount available for investment in Midland Bank Unit Trusts	£1 050.00
Number of units bought at say 50p each	2 100 units

The 'spread' between the bid and offer price for any unit trust is usually fixed at close to 6 % of the offer price, to cater for management charges and Stamp Duty.

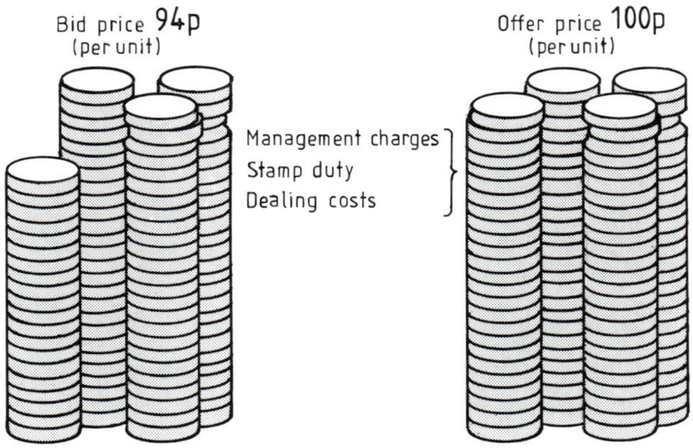

Form of Authority

To: Midland Bank Group Unit Trust Managers Limited, Freepost, Sheffield S1 1AY. Tel: 0742 769842

Number of shares or amount of stock	Name of company and details of stock

If there is insufficient space please attach a Continuation Sheet

I/We enclose certificates as listed above representing all the stock and shares to be exchanged
(Note: The relevant stock and share certificates must be in the possession of the Unit Trust Managers before any exchange can be made).
(Please remember that an exchange of shares for units is treated as a disposal for Capital Gains Tax purposes).
I/We authorise the exchange of the stock and shares listed above for Accumulation/Distribution+ Units in: —

Midland Bank ______________________ *Unit Trust(s)

+Delete which does not apply. *If no Trusts are specified your investment will be made in Midland Managed Portfolio

Minimum investment in any one Trust is £500

BLOCK LETTERS PLEASE

(1) Full Forename(s) ______________________ (Please state Mr., Mrs., Miss or Title)

Surname ______________________

Address ______________________

Postcode ______________________

Signature ______________________

Date ______________________

(2) Full Forename(s) ______________________ (Please state Mr., Mrs., Miss or Title)

Surname ______________________

Signature ______________________

SPECIMEN

I hold a Midland Bank
High Interest Cheque Account No: ☐☐☐☐☐☐☐☐ Agents stamp

Please tick box for details of:

☐ The range of Midland Bank Unit Trusts

☐ Regular Savings Plan ☐ Monthly Income Plan ☐ Midland Bank High Interest Cheque Account

(Midland Bank)

1 Answer the following questions on the text.

a What do the minimum amounts of £500.00 and £1,000.00 respectively mean to you?

b Which exchange scheme must be chosen if the bank is to grant a discount of 2 % on the offer price?

c What are your obligations if you order the bank to sell your shares?

2 Find adequate German translations. The short definitions will help you to get the meaning of the words.

a	*bid price*	what a buyer is willing to pay
b	*proceeds (of sale)*	money gained from the sale of something
c	*to allocate*	to give as a share
d	*offer price*	what a seller wants to get
e	*eligibility*	suitability for exchange; here, whether the shares are suitable for exchange
f	*contract note*	document for a transaction of shares
g	*valuation*	calculating how much money something is worth
h	*to surrender*	to give up possession of
i	*allotment*	number of shares allocated to an applicant for a new issue
j	*scrip issue*	free issue of shares given to existing shareholders
k	*rights issue*	right of existing shareholders to buy new shares in direct proportion to their holdings
l	*due to*	owing as a debt or right
m	*solicitor*	a lawyer who gives advice

3 Use the information given in the examples in the information sheet of Midland Bank (p. 75) to make a dialogue utilizing the following prompts:

Man: (comes to the counter, introduces himself and asks about Midland Bank Unit Trusts)
Clerk: (introduces himself, asks for the amount the customer wants to invest)
Man: (states a sum of £4,000.00 and mentions that he wants to exchange existing holdings for certificates because he wants more security)
Clerk: (asks for the number of shares and the names of the companies)
Man: (gives the required information)
Clerk: (tells the customer that his portfolio is suitable for investment in Midland Bank Unit Trusts)
Man: (asks for any special benefits he will have)
Clerk: (explains benefits: offer price instead of bid price, no expenses)
Man: (accepts the bank clerk's proposal)
Clerk: (asks his customer to fill in a Form of Authority)

Part F

Report: Investment policy and fund assets

The German share market profited in the first half of the year from the recovery of the US dollar as well as from expectations of positive company reports against the background of a generally buoyant economy. Aided by declining bond yields, the market moved steadily higher until the end of March, then suffered a sharp correction under the impact of rising interest rates. Towards the end of May, however, prices began to advance strongly again as interest rates eased and foreign investment capital flowed back into the German market. By mid-June the market had reached new heights for the year. The uptrend was accompanied by a sharp revival in trading volume from earlier depressed levels, enabling the broadly-traded blue chip issues in particular to register strong price gains by the end of June.

In CENTRAL, as a fund for German blue chips, our optimistic assessment of the German stock market prompted us to reduce the generally less volatile utility shares in the portfolio in favour of more price-sensitive issues. Here we concentrated our purchases in the banking sector as well as in the mechanical engineering area, where the positive earnings outlook holds out the potential of a good recovery in share prices following the sharp losses suffered last year.

(Translated from a leaflet by the German Investment Trust)

1 The text above was translated from German into English for a bank leaflet. Here are some passages of the German text, but not in the same order as in the English text. Find the corresponding English passages and state the line(s) from the English text passages matching the German text passages.

German text passages:

a Aktienmarkt
b positive Einschätzung der deutschen Börse
c Erleichterungen auf der Zinsseite
d sinkende Anleiherenditen
e Erholung des US-Dollars
f kursstabile Versorgungswerte
g ausgeprägte Kurskorrektur
h über Erwarten günstige Unternehmensberichte
i gute Ertragsperspektive
j gute gesamtwirtschaftliche Lage
k Rückkehr ausländischer Anlagegelder
l deutliche Aufwärtsbewegung des Marktes
m starke Kursverluste des Vorjahres
n Titel mit größerer Schwankungsbreite
o neue Jahreshöchststände
p Bereich Maschinenbau
q marktbreite Standardwerte

2 Translate the full English text into German using as many of the translations above as possible.

When you have done this compare your translation with the authentic German text which you will get from your teacher.

3 Translate the following short German text into adequate English.
Compare your translation with the translation you will get from your teacher.

German text:

Die Aktienmärkte werden wegen der günstigeren mittelfristigen Ertragsaussichten der Unternehmen auch künftig gute Anlagechancen bieten. Bei festverzinslichen Wertpapieren lassen Renditevorteile und zunehmende Stabilität im Devisenbereich die ausländischen Rentenmärkte im Vordergrund stehen. Wir haben uns in der Anlagepolitik für unsere Fonds frühzeitig auf diese Entwicklung eingestellt und sind deshalb überzeugt, daß sich die positive Entwicklung der Fonds auch in Zukunft fortsetzen wird.

Unit 14
Exchange rates always change

Part A

What is the most convenient way to send money abroad?

THE METHOD OF PAYMENT USED ABROAD

COUNTRY	CASH	CHEQUE	GIRO TRANSFER
AUSTRIA	✔	✔	✔
AUSTRALIA		✔	
BANGLADESH	✔		
BELGIUM	✔	✔	✔
CANADA		✔	
CYPRUS		✔	
DENMARK	✔	✔	✔
FINLAND	✔	✔	✔
FRANCE	✔	✔	✔
GERMANY	✔	✔	✔
GREECE		✔	
HONG KONG		✔	
ICELAND	✔		✔
INDIA	✔	✔	
IRISH REPUBLIC		✔	
ITALY		✔	✔
JAPAN	✔	✔	✔
LUXEMBOURG	✔	✔	✔
MALTA		✔	
MOROCCO	✔		
NETHERLANDS	✔	✔	✔
NEW ZEALAND		✔	
NORWAY	✔	✔	✔
PAKISTAN	✔		
PORTUGAL		✔	
SINGAPORE		✔	
SOUTH AFRIC		✔	
SPAIN	✔	✔	✔
SWEDEN	✔	✔	✔
SWITZERLAND	✔	✔	✔
THAILAND	✔		
TURKEY	✔	✔	
USA		✔	

(Girobank London)

In foreign trade or travel we have to change our money into the currency of the other country. The price we pay in our own money for the foreign money is the rate of exchange. Changes in demand and supply in the foreign exchange market cause fluctuations in the foreign exchange rate.

In 1960 the price for one US dollar was DM 4.1704, in 1980 the exchange rate was DM 1.8158 and in 1985 it increased again and DM 2.9424 had to be paid for one US dollar. In 1990 the rate for one US dollar fell to DM 1.6132 again.

Answer these questions.

1. Do you know what the currencies of the different countries are called?
2. What do you think is the best method of payment for sending money abroad?
3. What were the reasons for the ups and downs of the US$ in the past decades?

Part B

What exchange rates mean for exporters

When firms export goods, gains and losses can occur because of changes in the exchange rate of a currency.

For example, on 1 September a UK exporter sells a machine to Germany for 950.00 pounds. On that day the rate of exchange is 1 pound = 3 marks so the exporter fixes the contract price at 2,850.00 marks. Now assume that payment of 2,850.00 marks is made to the exporter on 1 November and that between 1 September and 1 November the pound could either have increased in value (appreciated), or decreased in value (depreciated).

Losses/gains resulting from changing exchange rates

Exchange rate of £1	£1 = 4.00 marks	£1 = 2.00 marks
Contract price	2,850.00 marks	2,850.00 marks
Sterling equivalent	£712.50	£1,425.00
Sterling gain/loss	**loss** of 950.00–712.50 = £237.50	**gain** of 1,425.00–950.00 = £475.00

The chart shows that an exporter can lose, in terms of sterling, if the pound appreciates. To prevent such a loss the exporter could:

– fix the contract price in terms of sterling so that payment of £950.00 would be received whatever the exchange rate on 1 November,

– sell marks forward. By using a forward selling contract the exporter could agree, on 1 September, to sell 2,850.00 marks on 1 November at an exchange rate agreed upon the September date. The exporter will then know precisely the amount of sterling which he will receive on 1 November even if the pound changes value in the meantime. The cost of arranging the forward contract can be considered to be a form of insurance premium. Forward dealing on foreign exchange markets, as described above, is very similar to forward dealing on commodity exchanges.

(Adapted from: Lett's Study Aids, s.a.)

1. Answer the following questions.

   a What is the foreign exchange rate and why is it a special problem for exporters?
   b What may lead to an increase in value of a certain currency?
   c How can exporters or importers eliminate the exchange risk in their foreign trade?

2 Which of the following statements about the rate of exchange is not true?

a The rate of exchange is the price of one currency expressed in terms of another currency.

b Changes in demand and supply lead to fluctuations of the foreign exchange rates.

c The appreciation of a currency is the increase in value of that currency.

d A forward contract fixes the rate at which a future sale or purchase will be effected.

e Currencies have to be changed in overseas trade because importers and exporters use the same currency.

3 Translate.

a Ein System der festen Wechselkurse entstand 1946 als Folge der Vereinbarungen von Bretton Woods, als der Internationale Währungsfonds (IWF) gegründet wurde.

b Es legte feste Paritäten zum Dollar fest, ließ aber kleine Abweichungen bis zu 2,25 % nach beiden Seiten zu.

c Um die Kurve stabil zu halten, mußten die Zentralbanken eingreifen, wenn die untere oder obere Grenze erreicht war.

Interventions of the Central Bank in a system of fixed parities to the US-Dollar

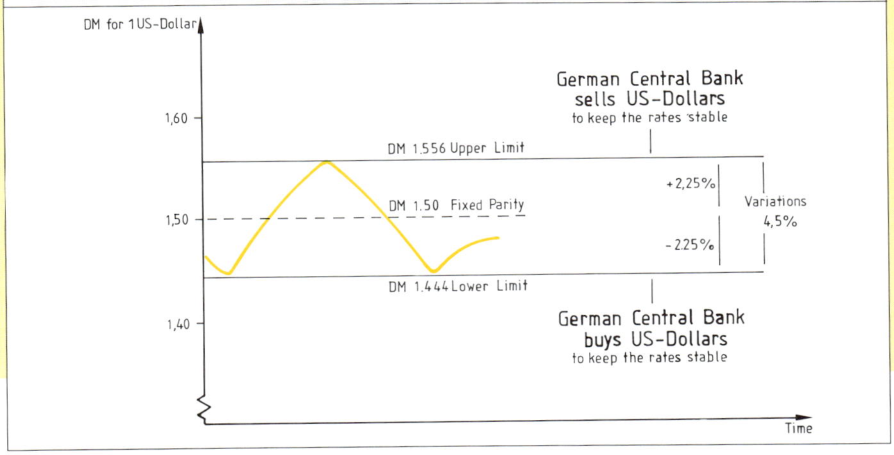

d Dieses System funktionierte bis zum Ende der sechziger Jahre, als der Dollar wegen eines ständigen Zahlungsbilanzdefizits unter Druck kam.

e Dies führte am Ende zu einer Abwertung des Dollars und einer Neubewertung der DM und einiger anderer Währungen.

f Die meisten Industrienationen gaben in den siebziger Jahren ihre festen Wechselkurse auf und ließen freie Kurse zu.

g Unter diesem neuen System werden die Wechselkurse durch Angebot und Nachfrage bestimmt, aber die Zentralbanken greifen noch ein in Fällen extremer Schwankungen.

h Einige Länder praktizieren noch eine mehr oder weniger strenge Form der Wechselkontrolle aus, mit Beschränkungen für Kapitalbewegungen und Reisedevisen.

i Wenn es keine Beschränkungen dieser Art gibt, sprechen wir von voller Konvertierbarkeit, das heißt, die Inlandswährung kann in jede andere Währung gewechselt werden und umgekehrt.

How exchange rates influence foreign trade

1 Foreign trade and exchange rates: Copy the list and fill in the missing words.

Country A	Country B
(e. g. Great Britain)	(e. g. Germany)
high rate of inflation	low rate of inflation
↓	↓
____________	export increases,
____________	import decreases
↓	↓
rate of exchange to currency B increases	____________
	____________
↓	↓
export decreases,	____________
____________	import increases

2 Sudden changes of the rate of exchange may have positive or negative effects on foreign trade:

A depreciation of important currencies have the following effects on German economy:

Export is more expensive

Consequences:
- less export
- countercyclical effects
- more unemployment

Import is cheaper

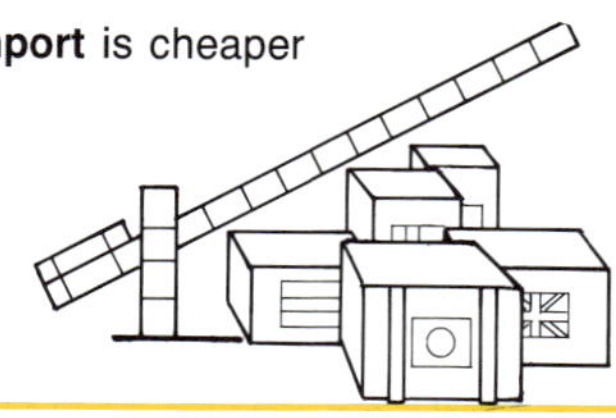

Consequences:
- more competition with other countries (unemployment)
- more stability in prices
- travelling to foreign countries is cheaper

Pairwork:

a Discuss with one of your classmates the consequences of a depreciation of the US$ for the German economy.

b What are the possible consequences of an appreciation of the French franc for the German economy?

A single currency before the year 2000?

There is a good chance that Europeans will have the ecu as their single currency before the year 2000. The 12 EC Member States started out on Stage I of EMU at the beginning of July 1990. The main aims during Stage I were to remove most of the remaining controls on money transactions and capital movements, and to achieve closer coordination of Member States' economic and budgetary policies and greater cooperation between central banks, the guardians of the value of money.

There are many reasons for creating a single European currency. It would eliminate exchange costs, promote trade and generate welfare gains. Not until monetary union has been achieved can the internal market, which was fully established in 1993, when all frontier controls were abolished, produce its full effects. A single European currency would also make for greater influence and stability in relation to the US dollar and the Japanese yen, which are often subject to wide exchange rate fluctuations. Moreover, a European currency has a symbolic importance in a growing Community which is becoming increasingly attractive to more and more countries.

A majority of EC residents are in favour of a single currency. The private sector too has for some time now demonstrated its support for the ecu as the European currency by launching initiatives of its own.

Ecu rate,
annual averages
ECU 1 =

Member State	1980	1990
B/L	40.6	42.4
DK	7.8	7.9
D	2.5	2.1
Gr	59.3	201.4
E	99.7	129.3
F	5.9	6.9
IRL	0.7	0.8
I	1 189.2	1 521.9
NL	2.8	2.3
P	69.6	181.1
UK	0.6	0.7

1 Diskuss the pros and cons of a single currency for Europe.

Unit 15
Trade terms and documents

Part A

Functions of trade terms

Main function

"In present international custom the main purpose of trade terms is to determine at what points the seller has fulfilled his obligations so that the goods in a legal sense could be said to have been delivered to the buyer."

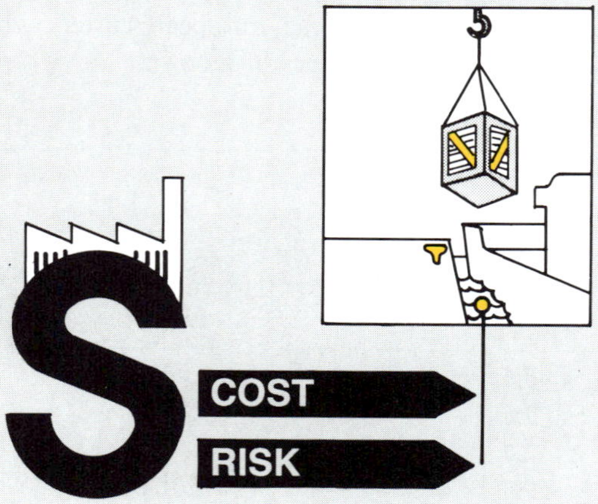

Secondary functions

The duty to provide export and import licences.

The nature and type of documents.

The extent of insurance protection.

The duty to pay for checking operations.

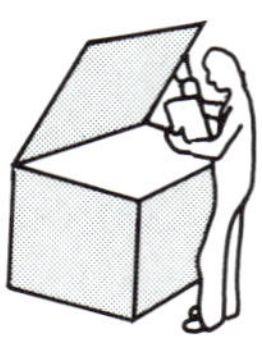

The duty to pack the goods.

The duty to notify the other party of any arrangements made.

In every international trade transaction certain questions must be answered:
- who will arrange and pay for the carriage of the goods from one point to another?
- who will bear the risk if these operations cannot be carried out?
- and who will bear the risk of loss of or damage to the goods in transit?

What do you know about the main and secondary functions of trade terms? Answer these questions referring to the charts.

a Who bears cost and risk when "ex works" was agreed upon?
b Why is an export licence sometimes required?
c Which documents do you know?
d Who pays for insurance in the German domestic market according to trade law?
e What does "notify" mean?
f Who is usually responsible for packing?
g Why are checking operations often necessary?

(Adapted from: Guide to Incoterms, International Chamber of Commerce, Paris)

The thirteen Incoterms

Part B

Ex works (EXW)
"Ex works" means that the seller's only responsibility is to make the goods available at his premises.

Free on board (FOB)
The goods are placed on board of a ship by the seller at a port of shipment named in the sales contract. The risk of loss of or damage to the goods is transferred from the seller to the buyer when the goods pass the ship's rail.

Free carrier (FCA)
This term has been designed to meet the requirements of modern transport, particularly such "multimodal" transport as container or "roll on – roll off" traffic by trailers and ferries. It is based on the same main principle as FOB except that the seller fulfills his obligations when he delivers the goods into the custody of the carrier at the named point.

Free alongside ship (FAS)
Under this term the seller's obligations are fulfilled when the goods have been placed alongside the ship on the quay or in lighters. It should be noted that, unlike FOB, the present term requires the buyer to clear the goods.

Cost and freight (CFR)
The seller must pay the costs and freight necessary to bring the goods to the named destination but the risk is transferred from the seller to the buyer when the goods pass the ship's rail in the port of shipment.

Cost, insurance and freight (CIF)
This term is basically the same as CFR but with the addition that the seller has to procure marine insurance against the risk of loss of or damage to the goods during the carriage.

Carriage paid to (CPT)
The seller pays the freight for the carriage of the goods to the named destination. However, the risk is transferred from the seller to the buyer when the goods have been delivered into the custody of the first carrier and not at the ship's rail.

Carriage and insurance paid to (CIP)
This term is the same as CPT but with the addition that the seller has to procure transport insurance against the risk of loss of or damage to the goods during the carriage.

Delivered ex ship (DES)
"Delivered ex ship" means that the seller shall make the goods available to the buyer on board the ship at the destination named in the sales contract. The seller has to bear the full cost and risk involved in bringing the goods there.

Delivered ex quay (DEQ)
This term is the same as DES with the exception that the goods must be made available to the buyer on the quay or wharf at the port of destination. There are two "Delivered ex quay" contracts in use, namely "Delivered ex quay (duty paid)" and "Delivered ex quay (duties on buyer's account)" in which the liability to clear the goods for import are to be met by the buyer instead of the seller.

Delivered at frontier (DAF)
The seller's obligations are fulfilled when the goods have arrived at the frontier – but before "the customs border" of the country named in the sales contract.

Delivered duty paid (DDP)
While the term "Ex works" signifies the seller's minimum obligation, the term "Delivery duty paid", when followed by words naming the buyer's premises, denotes the other extreme – the seller's maximum obligation.

Delivered duty unpaid (DDU)
The seller delivers the goods to the purchaser, who is responsible for paying any customs duties.

(Guide to Incoterms, s.a.)

1 What are the German translations of the thirteen Incoterms?

2

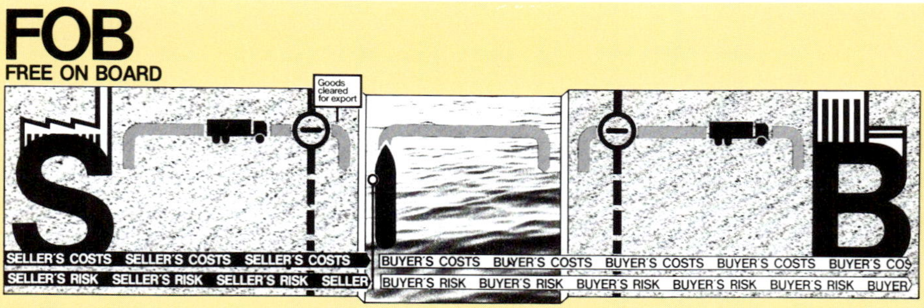

Are these buyer's or seller's duties when FOB is agreed upon?

a Provide export licence and pay export taxes and fees if required.
b Pay unloading costs.
c Pay loading costs according to the custom of the port to the extent that they are not included in the freight.
d Contract for the carriage and pay the freight.
e Nominate carrier.
f Deliver the goods on board.
g Pay loading costs to the extent that they are included in the freight.
h Provide a clean on board receipt.

3

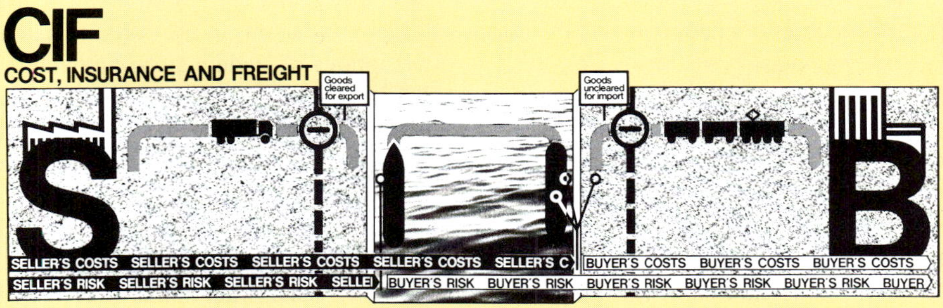

Are these buyer's or seller's duties when CIF is agreed upon?

a Contract for the insurance of the goods during the carriage and pay the insurance premium.
b Contract for the carriage and pay the freight to the named port of destination.
c Obtain export licence and pay export taxes and fees if required.
d Pay unloading costs to the extent that they are not included in the freight.
e Pay unloading costs to the extent that they are included in the freight.
f Pay loading costs.
g Furnish to the buyer the invoice, a clean bill of lading and a cargo insurance policy or certificate.
h Accept delivery of goods upon shipment when the documents have been tendered to him.

Choice of terms

Part C

At first glance, it would seem best that each of the contracting parties limits its obligation as much as possible. The seller would then try to negotiate an Ex Works contract while the buyer would try to convince the seller to deliver the goods duty paid to the buyer's premises.

In practice, however, the situation is not that simple. A seller or a buyer cannot simply make a better contract merely by shifting functions, costs and risks to the other contracting party.

The parties involved will probably be guided by the following criteria.

Market situation

In a highly competitive market, the seller may wish to offer prices to the buyer that are comparable to prices offered in the buyer's domestic market. The seller would then undertake to deliver the goods using terms such as "Delivered ex quay" or "Delivered Duty Paid". As a minimum the seller would be obliged to arrange and pay for transportation by using such terms as "CFR", "CIF", "Freight or Carriage Paid to" or "Freight or Carriage and Insurance Paid to". One should remember that additional costs and risks accepted by the seller are always reflected in the price.

Control of transport and insurance

In some instances an exporter of large and regular volumes of goods will usually be in a position to obtain better terms from carriers and insurers than the "occasional" importer. It may, furthermore, be comparatively simple to arrange the transport in the country of exportation and the risk of something going wrong will be minimal. In such cases there is really no reason why the seller should limit his obligations under an Ex Works, FAS, FOB or FCA agreement.

Sellers and buyers are not always prepared to accept risk of loss of and damage to the goods, or the risk of cost increases or circumstances hindering transport, in a foreign country. Under normal conditions of trade between countries with well-organised container ports and comparatively peaceful labour conditions, the risk of political disturbances, congestions in the ports, strikes or interruptions of trade may be minimal.

In such cases, the seller may be prepared to assume the risk during transport, and to choose a term in which his responsibilities extend to the arrival of the goods at the destination (Delivered ex ship, Delivered ex quay, Delivered At Frontier and Delivered Duty Paid). A seller who thinks that such risks may be difficult to ascertain and therefore difficult to include in the calculation of the price might prefer to have the buyer assume the risks during international transport. The well-known terms "FAS", "FOB", "CFR", "CPT" and the new term "FCA" all belong to this category. *(Guide to Incoterms, s.a.)*

1 Read the short definitions and find adequate German translations.

a	*at first glance*	your first impression when you look at something
b	*contracting (parties)*	(parties) having made a formal agreement
c	*to negotiate*	to produce an agreement
d	*premises*	building with surrounding land
e	*involved*	being concerned
f	*competitive*	when there is rivalry
g	*comparable*	that is similar
h	*domestic market*	market within a particular country
i	*obtain*	to get something by effort
j	*carrier*	a business firm transporting goods
k	*insurer*	a business firm taking over risks
l	*increase*	a rise in amount
m	*circumstances*	events influencing actions
n	*labour conditions*	situation of working people in business firms
o	*disturbances*	events threatening the usual way of life
p	*congestion*	overcrowded because of too much traffic
q	*to ascertain*	to make certain

2 Answer the following questions on the text.

a What are the two main criteria for the choice of Incoterms?
b In which market situation are terms like "DEQ" or "DDP" advisable for the seller?
c Are there economic reasons for the seller to offer terms like CIF or CIP?
d Which terms are suitable if the seller is willing to take over the risk during transport?
e What are possible risks that might affect trade between countries?
f Which terms mean that the buyer bears the risk during international transport?

The bill of lading – key to goods

The seller must furnish to the buyer a **clean, negotiable on board bill of lading** covering the transport to the agreed port of destination.

On board means that a so-called received for shipment bill of lading is not sufficient. If a received for shipment form of bill of lading has been used, it has to be "converted" into a shipped on board bill of lading by the words "shipped on board" stamped on the bill of lading by the carrier or by someone authorized by him to do so.

The word *clean* means that the bill of lading must not bear any superimposed clause or notation which expressly declares a defective condition of the goods or the packaging.

The word *negotiable* means that the goods will be delivered to the holder of the original of the bill of lading, when it is surrendered to the carrier. This means, that the buyer, in his turn, may sell the goods to another buyer pending their arrival at the destination.

The *bill of lading* is the carrier's receipt for the goods which also evidences the terms of the contract of carriage. The CFR buyer does not receive the goods themselves at the point of delivery. By the possession of the bill of lading, however, he is given a right to claim the goods from the carrier or, if the goods have been damaged or lost, compensation according to the terms of the contract. The right of compensation from the carrier is usually limited by means of exceptions and limitations of the amounts recoverable.

(Guide to Incoterms, s. a.)

1 Read the short definitions and find adequate German translations.

a	*to furnish*	to send
b	*to cover*	to refer to
c	*to convert*	to change
d	*superimposed clause*	additional remark
e	*notation*	written signs
f	*defective condition*	bad state
g	*to surrender*	to give to
h	*carrier*	business firm transporting goods
i	*pending*	while waiting for
j	*to evidence*	to prove something
k	*to claim the goods*	to request merchandise
l	*to claim compensation*	to request money for a loss or damage
m	*amounts recoverable*	money that can be obtained for a compensation

2 Find German translations for these words explained in the text:

a on board,
b clean,
c negotiable.

3 Why is the B/L the key to goods?

Insurance terms

The buyer, in case of loss of or damage to the goods, normally turns to the insurer. The insured amount is the CIF price plus 10 percent.

The extent of the cover for risks of loss of or damage to the goods varies under different terms of insurance. CIF is based on the principle of minimum liability for the seller, who only has to procure an insurance on so-called F.P.A. ("Free from particular average") terms. This means that the insurer is "free" and does not have to pay in case of partial loss or damage. Owing to this limitation the F.P.A. insurer only has to pay when incidents occur such as strandings, collisions and fire. Sometimes the shipper is called upon to pay contributions to the sea carrier for such costs which may have been incurred on account of extraordinary measures to save the ship and cargo from a common danger (e.g. costs for salvage or expenses in ports of rescue), so-called general average expenditure. In this case the F.P.A. insurer will cover his liability and deliver "general average bonds", which may be necessary to tender to the sea carrier in order to have the cargo released.

The F.P.A. insurance is really only sufficient for rough cargoes such as iron ore or coal. Fragile or valuable goods that may be particularly liable to damage or theft require more intensive insurance cover. This is usually achieved through a so-called "All Risks" policy. The extent of the cover may vary but the policy covers in principle all risks of fortuitous loss or damage to insured cargo from the time the goods leave the seller's warehouse until they reach the warehouse at the agreed destination.

In view of the limited protection offered by the F.P.A. terms, it is important that the CIF buyer, when the contract is made, requests the CIF seller to get more extensive cover whenever necessary.

This is customarily also done with respect to some special risks which are excluded in the ordinary insurance policy but which could be re-introduced by special clauses, such as war and strikes, riots and civil commotion clauses.

(Guide to Incoterms, s. a.)

1 Find adequate German translations. The short definitions will help you to get the meaning of the words.

a	*cover for risks*	insurance against loss, damage, etc.
b	*liability*	what you owe to somebody
c	*to procure*	to obtain by careful attention
d	*average*	loss or damage to a ship
e	*incident*	an unusual event
f	*salvage*	saving a wrecked ship
g	*port of rescue*	harbour where a damaged ship is taken
h	*to tender*	to offer as compensation
i	*to release*	to set free
j	*fragile*	easily broken or damaged
k	*fortuitous*	by accident
l	*customarily*	usually
m	*riots*	violent behaviour by a crowd of people
n	*civil commotion*	excited behaviour of people

2 Answer the following questions on the text.

a What is the insured amount for an insurance policy on F.P.A. terms?
b What is the limitation in the insurance cover on F.P.A. terms?
c What are "general average bonds" needed for?
d What is the extent of the cover offered by an "All Risks" policy?
e What are the special risks normally excluded in the ordinary insurance policy?

3 Make sure that you understand the following terms. Look them up in a dictionary if necessary.

a insurer
b insured (person)
c insurance premium
d insurance cover
e insurance claim
f insurance agent
g insurance broker
h (open) insurance policy
i insurance certificate

What you should remember about documents and trade terms

Part F

1 What are the German equivalents of these documents?

Transport documents:

a Bill of Lading (B/L)
b Mate's Receipt (M/R)
c Delivery Order (D/O)
d Consignment Note (CMR Waybill)
e Railroad Waybill
f Air Waybill

Warehousing and storage documents:

g Warehouse Warrant, Wharfinger's Warrant
h Dock Warrant

Insurance documents:

i Insurance Policy
j Insurance Certificate

Customs documents:

k Consular Invoice
l Certificate of Origin

2 Which of the documents mentioned in F1 are required if one of the following trade terms has been agreed upon?

a Ex works
b FAS
c CFR
d CIF
e DEQ
f DDP

3 What is the difference between an Insurance Policy and an Insurance Certificate?

4 Under which circumstances does an importer ask for a Consular Invoice?

5 Why is a Certificate of Origin often needed in international trade?

Unit 16
Financing by documentary letter of credit

Part A Application for documentary credit

JOAN'S BOUTIQUE

14 Charlotte Street, London W.C. 36

JB

The Manager
Commerzbank Aktiengesellschaft
London Branch
10-11 Austin Friars
London EC2N 2HE

20 March 19..

Dear Sir or Madam,

Please open an irrevocable documentary credit for HK$ 10,000.00 in favour of The Eastern Trading Company, Hong Kong. I have enclosed your application form with all the relevant details completed.

Please inform me when you have made arrangements with your agents in Hong Kong. Thank you.

Yours faithfully,

Joan Perrington

Joan Perrington
Manager Joan's Boutique

Encl. Application for documentary credit

COMMERZBANK AG – London Branch

APPLICATION FOR DOCUMENTARY CREDIT

DATE: 25 March 19..

Please open for our account a Documentary Credit, in accordance with the undermentioned particulars.

TYPE OF CREDIT:	Irrevocable
METHOD OF ADVICE:	airmail
ADVISING BANK:	Bank "X", Hong Kong
BENEFICIARY:	The Eastern Trading Company, 29, London Road, Hong Kong
AMOUNT:	HK$ 10,000.00 say ten thousand Hong Kong dollars
AVAILABILITY:	Valid until 30 June 19.. in Hong Kong for payment The credit is available by drafts drawn at 90 days sight accompanied by the required documents
DOCUMENTS:	Commercial invoice in three copies Air consignment note marked "Freight Paid" Packing list in triplicate Insurance certificate arranged by Joan's Boutique
GOODS:	Ladies dresses according to Order Number 35
TERMS:	CFR London
DISPATCH:	From Hong Kong to Heathrow Airport, London
PRESENTATION OF DOCUMENTS:	For acceptance within 7 days of the date of issue of the shipping documents
SIGNATURE:	Joan Perrington Joan Perrington Joan's Boutique, London

Answer the following questions on the above application for a documentary credit.

1 Who is the importer of the ladies' dresses?

2 Who is the exporting firm?

3 Why is the exporter the beneficiary?

4 What is the role of Commerzbank AG – London Branch?

Notification of documentary credit

Landesbank Burgstadt

Anschrift/Address: Bahnhofstraße 23, Postfach/P. O. Box/BP 123, D - 9800 Überall
Telefon: (09 87) 4 56 71
Fernschreiber/Telex: 987 654
S.W.I.F.T.-Address: SUELL DE 99

IRREVOCABLE DOCUMENTARY CREDIT
UNWIDERRUFLICHES DOKUMENTEN-AKKREDITIV

Number – *Nummer*: 57500/468

Date and place of expiry – *Datum und Ort des Verfalls*: 31 May 19.. at counters of advising bank

Applicant – *Auftraggeber*:
Joan's Boutique
14 Charlotte Street
London W.C. 36

Beneficiary – *Begünstigter*:
The Eastern Trading Company
29, London Road
Hong Kong

Registered – *Einschreiben* – Recommandée

Advising Bank – *Avisierende Bank*: Bank "X", 35 Kings Road North, Hong Kong
Ref.No. – *Ref.-Nr.* 8536

Amount – *Betrag*: HK$ 10,000.00 (Hong Kong dollars ten thousand)

Credit available with – *Akkreditiv benutzbar bei*

Partial shipments – *Teilverladungen*: ☐ allowed *gestattet* ☒ not allowed *nicht gestattet*
Transhipment – *Umladung*: ☐ allowed *gestattet* ☒ not allowed *nicht gestattet*

by *durch*: ☐ sight payment *Sichtzahlung* ☒ acceptance *Akzeptleistung* ☐ negotiation *Negoziierung* ☐ deferred payment at *hinausgeschobene Zahlung*

Loading on board/dispatch/taking in charge from/at
Verladung/Versendung/Übernahme von/in: Hong Kong

for transportation to
zur Beförderung nach: Heathrow Airport, London

against presentation of the documents detailed herein
gegen Einreichung der nachstehend genannten Dokumente

☒ and beneficiary's draft at *und Tratte(n) des Begünstigten per*: 90 days sight
on *auf*: Bank "X", 35 Kings Road North Hong Kong

Documents to be presented:

SIGNED INVOICE IN THREE COPIES certifying that the goods are in accordance with Joan's Boutique Order Number 35 dated 14.02.19..

AIR CONSIGNMENT NOTE evidencing goods dispatched to Joan's Boutique, 14 Charlotte Street, London W.C. 36 marked "Freight Paid"

PACKING LIST IN TRIPLICATE

We are informed that insurance is being arranged by our principals.

Covering Ladies Dresses
CFR Heathrow Airport, London

Documents to be presented within days after the date of issuance of the shipping document(s) but within the validity of the credit.
Die Dokumente sind innerhalb von Tagen nach dem Ausstellungsdatum des (der) Verladedokumente(s) vorzulegen, jedoch innerhalb der Gültigkeitsdauer des Akkreditivs.

We hereby issue this Documentary Credit in your favour. It is subject to the Uniform Customs and Practice for Documentary Credits (1983 Revision, International Chamber of Commerce, Publication No. 400) and engages us in accordance with the terms thereof, and especially in accordance with the terms of Article 10 thereof. The number and the date of the credit and the name of our bank must be quoted on all drafts required. If the credit is available by negotiation, each presentation must be noted on the reverse of this advice by the bank where the credit is available.

Wir eröffnen hiermit dieses Dokumenten-Akkreditiv zu Ihren Gunsten. Es unterliegt den Einheitlichen Richtlinien und Gebräuchen für Dokumenten-Akkreditive (Revision 1983, Internationale Handelskammer, Publikation Nr. 400), und verpflichtet uns gemäß deren Bestimmungen, insbesondere gemäß Artikel 10. Nummer und Eröffnungsdatum des Akkreditivs sowie der Name unserer Bank sind auf allen geforderten Tratten anzugeben. Falls das Akkreditiv durch Negoziierung benutzbar ist, muß jede Inanspruchnahme von der Bank, bei der das Akkreditiv benutzbar ist, auf der Rückseite dieser Ausfertigung vermerkt werden.

This document consists of signed page(s).
Dieses Dokument besteht aus unterschriebenen Seite(n).

Advice for the beneficiary / *Ausfertigung für den Begünstigten*

147 110 (1) (Fassung Febr. 88) 2/88
Deutscher Sparkassenverlag

1 Why do certain documents have to be presented to the importer's bank?

2 Look at the following definitions of documents used in foreign trade.
What are the names of these documents?
Write these names and their German translations in your vocabulary note-book.

a a document demanding payment for goods and services
b an instruction from a banker to a foreign bank authorizing the payment of money to the firm named in the letter
c a written order from one person (the drawer) to another (the drawee) requiring the drawee to pay a specified sum
d a document showing the name of the country from which a shipment of goods has originated
e a document made out by a person who sends goods by air freight
f a document entitling a buyer of goods the right to claim them from a ship
g a special invoice, legalized by a consul, that is sometimes required by the customs of an importing country
h a note accompanying the goods delivered and giving details

3 Find out the meaning of the following abbreviations of Incoterms. Write short definitions in your note-book.

a FOB **b** FAS **c** CFR **d** CIF **e** DEQ **f** Ex works

Part C

Exporter to agent bank

THE EASTERN TRADING COMPANY

29, LONDON ROAD, HONG KONG

The Manager
Bank "X"
35 Kings Road North
Hong Kong

05 May 19..

Dear Sir or Madam,

Thank you for your advice of 22 April. We have now effected shipment to our customers in London and enclose the shipping documents you asked for and our draft for HK$ 10,000.00.

Will you please accept the draft and remit the proceeds to our account at the Hong Kong International Bank, Kow Loon.

Yours faithfully,

Ken Renfrew

Ken Renfrew
Finance Manager

Encs.
Commercial Invoice CFR Heathrow Airport London (three copies)
Air Consignment Note
Packing List in Triplicate
Draft No. 243/KR

Answer the following questions.

1. What do you think was in the letter of Bank "X" to The Eastern Trading Company dated from 22 April?
2. What does The Eastern Trading Company write to Joan's Boutique?
3. What does Bank "X" write to Commerzbank AG – London Branch?

Part D

Issuing bank to importer

COMMERZBANK AG – London Branch

Mrs Joan Perrington
Joan's Boutique
14 Charlotte Street
London W.C. 36

12 May 19..

Dear Mrs Perrington,

In accordance with your instructions of 20 March our agents, Bank "X", Hong Kong, accepted a draft for HK$ 10,000.00 drawn by The Eastern Trading Company on presentation of shipping documents sent to you on 05 May.

We have debited your account with the amount of HK$ 10,000.00 plus our charges of £ 29.00 Sterling. The documents are now with us and will be handed to you when you call.

Yours sincerely,

Franz Viehbacher

Franz Viehbacher
Manager

- When should Mrs Perrington call for the documents?

Procedure of a documentary letter of credit

Here are ten paragraphs describing the stages in an irrevocable documentary credit transaction. They are in the wrong order. It is your task to think about the right order. Write the numbers of the paragraphs in their correct order on your own sheet of paper.

Paragraphs in wrong order:

Situation: Goods exported from Germany to USA

(1) The importer's bank notifies German bank about the matter and sends full details of the letter of credit and asks the bank to confirm the credit.

(2) The exporter and importer agree on payment by irrevocable and confirmed documentary credit.

(3) German bank settles account with US bank and sends the documents.

(4) The importer instructs his bank to arrange an irrevocable and confirmed documentary credit in favour of the exporter. He details the goods required and the arrangements the exporter must make.

(5) On receipt of the documents the US bank debits the importer's account with the amount of the credit plus expenses and releases documents to the importer.

(6) German bank notifies the exporter that the credit is open by means of a letter of credit. It also sends its confirmation of the letter of credit.

(7) The exporter presents documents to German bank. Bank examines documents, and if in conformity with terms of credit, pays the exporter's draft.

(8) The exporter manufactures or obtains the goods, and ships them exactly as required in the letter of credit, receiving in turn an air waybill or bill of lading.

(9) Importer uses documents to release goods from the shipping company and customs.

(10) The goods leave the port of shipment en route to the port of destination.

Vocabulary according to units

Unit 1

accommodation Unterkunft
If you don't live at home you have to find accommodation on the private market.

anticipation Erwartung
The first salary at the end of the month will be awaited with joyful anticipation.

apprenticeship Lehrzeit
My apprenticeship lasts for two and a half years.

block release Blockunterricht
I will attend the vocational school on block release.

branch Zweigstelle
I worked in the cheque department of a local branch of my bank.

career opportunities Aufstiegschancen
What career opportunities are open to you after your apprenticeship?

cheque department Scheckabteilung
Before the first block release course I worked in the cheque department of my bank.

commute pendeln
Many people who have to commute to their place of work take a bus.

corporate sector Unternehmenssektor
The merchant banks deal mainly with the corporate sector.

credit cooperative Kreditgenossenschaft
Most credit cooperatives were founded in the rural areas of a country.

day release Teilzeitunterricht
Some of my former classmates attended the vocational school on day release.

discount Preisnachlaß
Buses are cheap and there are usually discounts to be obtained on a monthly basis.

gross salary Bruttogehalt
After deductions for social security and taxes about two thirds of my gross salary are left to spend.

head office Hauptstelle
Most finance experts of our bank work in the head office.

investment adviser Anlageberater
After my apprenticeship I want to specialize as an investment adviser.

join a bank in eine Bank eintreten
I joined the savings bank on 1st September.

local head office Filiale
There are 10 local head offices of our bank in Germany.

maintenance Unterhalt
Using a car is very expensive because of costs for petrol and maintenance.

monetary policy Geldpolitik
Does the Bank of England carry out the government's monetary policy?

MOT TÜV
The costs for MOT tests and MOT certificates have increased in the past years.

municipal savings bank Stadtsparkasse
The general manager of a municipal savings bank is elected by the council of a community.

nationalize verstaatlichen
The Bank of England was nationalized in 1946.

note issue Ausgabe von Banknoten
The central bank is responsible for the note issue.

public-law credit institution öffentlich-rechtliches Kreditinstitut
All the profits of a public-law credit institution have to be paid to the community.

registered office Verwaltungszentrale
The German central bank has its registered office in Frankfurt.

related verwandt
The bank specialised in providing payments and related services.

securities depository bank Pfandbriefbank
Securities depository banks specialise in financing in the long run.

staff Belegschaft
Employers often insist that the staff dress in a particular way.

subsidiary Tochtergesellschaft
The bank I work at has also a subsidiary in London.

superannuation Rentenbeiträge
The basic deductions of my gross salary are tax and superannuation.

trustee savings bank öffentlich-rechtliche Sparkasse
Trustee savings banks serve mainly the personal sector.

vocational school Berufsschule
My lessons at the vocational school are part of my training on the job.

Unit 2

abbreviation Abkürzung
What does the abbreviation VAT stand for?

application form Antragsformular
Now that we have discussed everything let us fill in this application form.

balance Saldo
You get a half per cent for a positive balance on your account.

basic charge Grundgebühr
Many banks debit a basic charge per month regardless of the number of transactions.

cash dispenser Geldautomat
It is a machine from which you can get money by using a cash card in connection with an identification number.

connection Verbindung
We offer a lot of extra services in connection with a current account.

Unit 2

credit Guthaben
Can you tell me what the entries on the credit side of my account mean?

current account Girokonto
With a current account you can pay in money, withdraw money and transfer money.

debit Schuld
How many entries are on the debit side of my account?

direct debit Lastschrift
For payments with variable amounts like telephone bills our direct debit system can be used.

fee Gebühr
If you want to have Eurocheques you have to pay an additional fee to your bank.

interest Zins
How much interest do I get for my money on a savings account?

occupation Beschäftigung
Please state your present occupation and your employer's name.

overdraft Dispositionskredit
The overdraft you get from your bank depends on your regular salary.

overdraft facility Kreditrahmen
We can grant you an overdraft facility being three times more than the amount of your regular salary.

overdraw überziehen
You can overdraw your account up to a fixed limit.

paying-in slip Einzahlungsschein
With a paying-in slip you can prove that you have paid money into your account.

power of attorney Vollmacht
Do you want to give power of attorney to the junior manager?

remit überweisen
Have you already remitted this bill?

sign unterschreiben
Would you please sign here?

specimen signature Unterschriftsprobe
A specimen signature is the »photograph« by which the bank will recognize its account holder.

standing order Dauerauftrag
We offer standing orders for regular payments such as rent, hire purchase or insurance premiums.

statement Kontoauszug
Your statement informs you about movements on the credit and debit side of your account.

transfer überweisen
Your employer will transfer your salary to your account.

withdraw abheben
If you need cash you can withdraw money from your account.

Unit 3

actual tatsächlich
You must include the actual interest received in your return of total income.

advance interest Vorschußzins
You may withdraw money without giving notice but then advance interest will be charged.

advance notice rechtzeitige Kündigung
You must give advance notice if you want to withdraw larger amounts.

agreed period of notice vereinbarte Kündigungsfrist
You can choose an agreed period of notice ranging from six months to four years.

assess schätzen
Your tax will be assessed if you can't prove what you have earned.

basic rate income tax Basissteuer auf Zinserträge
You have to pay basic rate income tax for interest received on your bank account.

cheque account Girokonto
A current account or a cheque account is very convenient for an employee.

deposit account Sparkonto
If you have some money to spare then you could open a deposit account or a savings account.

discharge (Schulden) übernehmen
We will discharge the basic rate income tax on your interest.

gross up aufschlagen
The tax is assessed on the actual interest paid, grossed up at the basic rate.

Inland Revenue Finanzamt
The Inland Revenue collects national taxes in Britain.

interest received Zinsertrag
There is income tax deducted from the interest received on your account.

joint account Gemeinschaftskonto
Joint accounts are usually opened by husband and wife.

legal period of notice gesetzliche Kündigungsfrist
You may choose either a savings account with an agreed or with a legal period of notice.

loan account Darlehenskonto
When I bought my new car my loan account was debited with a fairly large amount of money.

particulars Einzelangaben
The bank supplies to the Inland Revenue particulars of interest paid or credited to investors.

reclaim zurückfordern
You cannot reclaim tax already paid by your bank.

return of total income Einkommensteuererklärung
You must make a return of total income to the Inland Revenue.

safe custody account Depotkonto
You can leave your valuables like jewelry or insurance policies in your bank's safe custody account.

share account Teilhaberkonto
As a holder of a share account, you are a member of the society.

time deposit account Festgeldkonto
We are recommending you a time deposit account for an investment of money in short term.

Unit 4

bank statement Kontoauszug
A bank statement informs about all the transactions on your account during a certain period of time.

beneficiary Begünstigter
Name and address of the beneficiary have to be filled in the form.

cash discount Skonto
Do you allow a cash discount if I will pay within two weeks?

cheque guarantee card Scheckkarte
With a cheque guarantee card the payment of cheques is guaranteed up to a certain amount.

code number Geheimzahl
Don't forget to fill in the code number of the beneficiary's bank.

counterfoil Kontrollabschnitt
The counterfoil is kept by the customer as evidence of payment.

designed for bestimmt für
The third part of a transfer form is designed for the beneficiary.

effect ausführen
The first part of the transfer form is the instruction to the payer's bank to effect the transfer.

evidence Beweis
The counterfoil of a paying-in slip is evidence that a certain sum of money has been paid.

multiple credit Sammelüberweisung
Providing the bank with a single cheque to cover the total wage bill is an example of multiple credits.

payee Zahlungsempfänger
The payee is credited by his bank on receipt of the credit form.

permit erlauben
With direct debiting the payee is permitted to debit the payer's account on a certain date.

provide versorgen mit
A firm provides its bank with a list of employees and their bank account numbers.

purchase kaufen
What do you want to purchase for this loan?

purpose Zweck
In a remittance you make a reference to the purpose of the payment.

receipt Quittung
The payee is credited by his bank on receipt of the credit form.

receipted quittiert
A receipted counterfoil is retained by the customer as evidence of in-payment or deposit.

remittance Überweisung
You have to use a remittance form to send money to another person's account.

request Verlangen
The bank is authorized to make any payment requested by a payee.

responsibility Verantwortung
With direct debiting it is the responsibility of the payee to inform the bank about the amount to be paid.

retain einbehalten
The second part of the transfer form is the copy to be retained by the customer.

specimen Muster
Look at this specimen form for a transfer order.

subscription Abonnement
You can use the direct debit system e.g. for a subscription to a newspaper.

supply liefern
We can supply you with goods of first-class quality.

value added tax (VAT) Mehrwertsteuer
How much is the net price, VAT and the total?

voucher Beleg
The first part of a transfer form serves as a debit voucher.

Unit 5

access Zugang
With a Eurocheque card you will have access to the electronic banking facilities of your bank.

account updating Aktualisierung der Konten
Using a computerised system account updating takes only a very short time.

automated teller machine (ATM) Selbstbedienungsbank
ATMs can provide customers with a range of services as well as simple cash dispensing.

bill Rechnung
Our service provides payment of bills up to 30 days in advance.

branch network Zweigstellennetz
Many banks having large branch networks are reluctant to move into the mass home banking market.

building society Bausparkasse
The Nottingham building society was among the first to introduce a home banking system for its customers.

cash management Finanzservice
A cash management module for small businesses is part of a homebanking system of some banks.

cashpoint card Automatenkarte
Inside the automated area of their bank the customers can use their cashpoint card to withdraw money and get information.

due to wegen
Due to public indifference there has not yet been established a mass home banking market.

electronic money transmission belegloser Zahlungsverkehr
BACS is an example for the system of electronic money transmission.

exchange of data media Datenträgeraustausch
Exchange of data media is part of the CHAPS system.

homebanking Homebanking
Although the technology is available to provide homebanking, the services at present provided are limited.

Unit 5

issue Ausgabe
With all ATMs, customers are issued a card and a PIN number.

lobby banking Bankdienste in Selbstbedienung
Lobby banking provides fully automated areas to which customers have access outside banking hours.

personal identification number (PIN) Persönliche Kennummer
With your exclusive PIN number you have access to many services of your bank.

Prestel Bildschirmtext
Prestel is the British equivalent to the German Bildschirmtext system.

query Frage
With the introduction of ATMs cashiers were freed to deal with more individual queries of customers.

reluctance Widerwillen
There is reluctance at present on the part of many banks to move into the mass home banking market.

service hall Schalterhalle
There are cash dispensers and ATMs in the service hall of a modern bank.

sophisticated hochentwickelt
One of the major developments of electronic banking is more sophisticated cash dispensing.

till Kasse
ATMs have now appeared inside the service hall of banks in an attempt to reduce queues at tills.

viewing facility Bildschirmauskunft
The system of homebanking offers also a viewing facility via TV of account transactions.

Unit 6

advise benachrichtigen
You must advise the bank if you change your signature.

apply beantragen
I'd like to apply for that credit card.

approximately ungefähr
Any cheque you write up to approximately 400 deutschmarks will be paid.

authorize ermächtigen
To fill in a cheque is to authorize the bank to pay out money from an account.

available verfügbar
A list of all banks which accept Eurocheques outside Europe is available at our branches.

bearer cheque Inhaberscheck
Bearer cheques can be passed on like a banknote.

benefit from Nutzen ziehen aus
These small businesses have benefited greatly from the fall in interest rates.

blank cheque Blankoscheck
Take this blank cheque and write in whatever amount you want to receive.

bounce platzen (Scheck)
You don't have to worry about whether your cheque might bounce.

claim Anspruch
A discount credit arises as a result of the buying of claims based on bills.

countermand widerrufen
Once you have filled in and signed the cheque you cannot countermand payment.

crossed cheque Verrechnungsscheck
Crossed cheques have two parallel lines on them and must be paid into an account.

currency Währung
Our network of cash dispensers makes local currency available 24 hours a day.

drawee Bezogener
The drawee is the person who has to pay a bill or a cheque.

drawer Aussteller
The drawer is the person who writes out a cheque or a bill.

endorsement Indossament
Order cheques can only be negotiated by endorsement.

equivalent Entsprechung
You can use your cheque to withdraw the equivalent of approximately 400 deutschmarks.

expire ablaufen
Has the Eurocheque card already expired?

fault Fehler
If cheques are stolen without a fault of the customer the bank will usually replace them free of charge.

genuine echt
For the most part discount transactions at the banks are based on genuine trade bills.

honour einlösen
Are you sure that the cheque will be honoured?

impeccable einwandfrei
Only bills of impeccable creditworthiness can be rediscounted.

liable for haftbar
The issuing bank shall not be liable for any Eurocheque that has been filled in with more than 400 deutschmarks.

negotiate weitergeben
Bearer cheques can be negotiated like a banknote.

notify benachrichtigen
If you notify your bank in due time lost cheques will be replaced.

open cheque Barscheck
With an open cheque you obtain cash from the drawee bank.

order cheque Orderscheck
Order cheques can only be negotiated by endorsement.

presenter Einreicher
The parties to a bill are called drawer, drawee and presenter.

proceeds Erlöse
Are the proceeds from the sale of these goods sufficient to cover the bill?

property Eigentum, Besitz
The card remains' the property of the issuing bank.

Unit 6

recipient Empfänger
Crossed cheques are safe and the recipient can always be traced back.

retailer Einzelhändler
A retailer sells goods in small quantities.

trace back zurückverfolgen
With crossed cheques the recipient can always be traced back.

Unit 7

abroad im Ausland
There are so many different ways to take money abroad.

back-up Unterstützung
Perhaps you need a backup to pay for any unexpected bills.

cancellation charges Rücktrittsgebühren
If you have to pay cancellation charges you can claim reimbursement from your insurance.

collect abholen
I wish to collect my travel facilities next Monday.

comprehensive umfassend
Many banks nowadays offer comprehensive travel services.

cover Versicherungsschutz gewähren
Do you have the right insurance to cover you or your car?

coverage Versicherungsschutz
The coverage for the different risks of travel varies from bank to bank.

credit card Kreditkarte
In some countries credit cards are accepted only in tourist areas.

denomination Stückelung
If you have a preference for one or more denominations please tick the appropriate box.

departure Abfahrt
There are those anxious hours as departure time approaches.

destination Bestimmungsort
If you take cheques in the currency of your destination, you will get a better rate of exchange.

disablement Behinderung
In the event of permanent disablement you get a reimbursement from your insurance.

excess commission Zusatzprovision
With cheques in the currency of your destination you can often avoid excess commission.

exchangeable einlösbar
You should have some readily exchangeable cheques for the cash you'll need during your stay.

foot bezahlen
You can enjoy your holiday to the full if it's not you who foots the bill.

hospital benefit Krankengeld
You get hospital benefit if you are admitted to hospital as an in-patient outside the UK.

ingredient Bestandteil
Money is one of the most important ingredients of a good trip.

insurance Versicherung
It's important to take out insurance well before setting off abroad.

liability Verpflichtung
Your insurance pays for legal liability in respect of third party damage.

medical expenses Arztkosten
Medical expenses are paid for if you become ill or have an accident.

odd gelegentlich
You need some cash for the odd meal or drink before you reach your final destination.

personal property persönlicher Besitz
If anything of your personal property is stolen or damaged you can get a reimbursement from your insurance.

pre-prepared aufliegend, verfügbar
Please write in the box how many of each pre-prepared pack of cheques you require.

premium Prämie
For a small premium the travel insurance can carry the risk.

refund ersetzen
If you ever lose your travellers' cheques, they can always be refunded.

reimburse Schadensersatz leisten
A travel insurance policy will reimburse you if you had extra costs because of a travel delay.

request form Antrag, Wunschliste
I need some information to fill out this travel services request form.

requirements Anforderungen
We will try to meet your requirements as closely as possible.

tip Trinkgeld geben
In many hotels there will be porters to tip.

travellers' cheque Reisescheck
Dollars, Swiss francs and deutschmarks are recommended currencies for travellers' cheques.

visa Visum
There are so many things to think of — tickets, passports, sometimes even visas to organise.

Unit 8

appropriate passend
Please cite the appropriate passage in the text.

attentive aufmerksam
You can count on our organization for attentive assistance.

availability Verfügbarkeit
Our services are subject to cash availability.

basically im Grunde
All credit cards are basically the same.

billing period Abrechnungszeitraum
The card holder receives a statement listing all payments made during the billing period.

client Kunde
Credit means the amount of money a bank places at a client's disposal.

Unit 8

convenience Bequemlichkeit
When you travel the card will bring you an extra measure of security and convenience.

disposal Verfügung
A bank places an amount of money at a client's disposal.

draw upon verfügen über
A client can draw upon the amount of money a finance company places at his disposal.

emergency Notfall
Our travel service offices help with travel plans and in case of an emergency.

establishment Niederlassung
Card issuing companies usually charge a fee for their service to participating business establishments.

finance charge Finanzierungsgebühr
There is no finance charge if the card holder pays the total bill.

inquire sich erkundigen
Please inquire about the Corporate Card Program for company management.

instalment Rate
If the cardholder pays in instalments he must pay at least the minimum shown on the statement.

judgment Beurteilung
Please find the passage in the text that supports your judgment.

keep track of auf dem laufenden bleiben
Cardmembers receive copies of all charges, which makes it easy to keep track of financial transactions.

occur auftreten
Put the statements in the same order as they occur in the text.

participate teilhaben
Many companies participate in the card issuing business.

pertinent to sachdienlich
All information pertinent to the transaction is filled out at the time of purchase.

record Aufzeichnung
We are providing signed copies of charges for easy record keeping.

rental Verleih
Most major car rentals and hotels welcome the Card.

resource Mittel, Potential
You are limited only by your ability to pay and your personal resources.

sales voucher Verkaufsbeleg
A sales voucher is filled out at the time of purchase.

subject to abhängig von
These services are subject to local regulations.

toll-free gebührenfrei
We are providing toll-free customer service for orders made by phone.

Unit 9

advance Vorschuß
When is the advance for that order due?

appointment Verabredung
I have an appointment with the manager at 10 o'clock.

assembly Zusammenbau, Montage
There are no extra charges for assembly and delivery.

assignment Forderungsabtretung
An assignment is a transfer of a claim by a creditor to a third party.

base rate Basiszinssatz
The interest is calculated daily and expressed as a percentage of the bank's base rate.

bill discounting Wechseldiskontierung
Bill discounting is one of the forms of a loan with personal security.

borrow ausleihen
Borrowing means taking money from a person with the understanding that it will be returned after a certain time.

commission Provision
A separate credit commission may be charged.

competitive wettbewerbsfähig
Our interest rates are very competitive.

cover Versicherungsschutz
I require Personal Loan Protector Cover to the first-named person above.

credit assessment Kreditprüfung
I authorize the bank to carry out a credit assessment by making third-party inquiries.

dead pledge Faustpfand
Movable objects are regarded as dead pledges in a lien.

default on payment Zahlungsverzug
In the case of default on payment the creditor can redeem his claim by selling off the lien.

dependent children unterhaltsberechtigte Kinder
Do you have to care for any dependent children?

estimate schätzen
What is the estimated value of your real estate?

fittings Einrichtungsgegenstände
Our decorating department can offer you a complete range of fittings.

fixtures Inventar
The price of the house includes the bathroom fixtures.

hire purchase Ratenkauf
In a hire purchase agreement the ownership of the property remains with the seller.

in case falls
I can prepare all the necessary forms in case you need a credit.

joint liability Mithaftung
Additional security may rest on joint liability through other parties.

land charge Grundschuld
No individual is held responsible for a land charge, only the land itself is the debt.

Unit 9

land register Grundbuch
Land cannot be transferred, but the title is evidenced in a public register, the land register.

lending period Darlehenslaufzeit
You can repay the loan in one sum at the end of the lending period.

liabilities Verbindlichkeiten
Are there any other liabilities you haven't mentioned so far?

lien Pfandrecht
A liability can be secured by a lien in the form of a physical object.

look up nachschlagen
I need your account number to look up your balance.

marital status Familienstand
Please state in the loan proposal your marital status.

match passen
We can offer you sofas and matching chairs.

mortgage Hypothek
A mortgage forms a contractual obligation with which it is inextricably linked.

option Wahlrecht
Interest is debited quarterly to the customer's account or at any other option of the customer.

overdraft Dispositionskredit
What is the difference between a personal loan and an overdraft?

owe schulden
With a personal loan the customer knows exactly how much he owes.

pay-as-you-earn (PAYE) Lohnsteuer
What is your net income after deduction of PAYE and national insurance stamps?

permanent residence ständiger Wohnsitz
Would you please tell me your permanent residence?

personal loan Persönlicher Kredit
It will be no problem for us to grant you a personal loan because you earn a good salary.

pledge verpfänden
Additional security may rest on the value of certain objects that the borrower pledges to his bank.

principal Darlehensbetrag
Our loans are repayable in equal monthly instalments of principal and interest.

real estate Grundbesitz
Mortgage liens are used for long-term real estate loans.

recommend empfehlen
We sell below prices recommended by manufacturers.

redeem zurückkaufen
The debtor can redeem his pledge by paying the owed sum of money.

refund erstatten
You will get the German VAT refunded.

repayment of principal Tilgung
An instalment consists of repayment of principal, interest and service charges.

sales staff Verkaufspersonal
Our friendly sales staff will advise you in your own language.

spouse Ehegatte
Sometimes liability of the customer's spouse is required.

supplier Lieferant
We are one of the largest suppliers of furniture.

surety Bürgschaft
Whoever takes on a surety, pledges himself to the creditor of a third party.

tenant Pächter
My residential status is being a tenant.

term of a loan Darlehenslaufzeit
Our interest rates are fixed throughout the term of the loan.

Unit 10

annual percentage rate (APR) Jahreszinssatz
If you can take out a secured loan this could result in lower APR than on unsecured loans.

appraisal fee Schätzgebühr
You have to pay an appraisal fee for assessing the value of a house.

asset Vermögen
If you have any assets that you can use as collateral you may be able to take out a secured loan.

closing costs Abschlußkosten
Closing costs vary according to the amount being borrowed.

collateral zusätzliche Sicherheit
You can use the equity built up over the years as collateral to secure a loan.

consolidate zusammenfassen
You may want to consolidate a number of smaller debts.

deferred taxation Steuerstundung
In a balance sheet you have to make a provision for deferred taxation.

depreciate im Wert sinken
The house's value will depreciate by about five per cent in the first year.

dividend stamp Dividendenanteil
The ratio of dividend stamps to trading surplus has increased in the past years.

down payment Anzahlung
There is no down payment necessary on new or used cars.

equity Eigenkapital
If you own your own home you can use the equity built up over the years to secure a loan.

expenses Kosten
Her company sent her to Berlin and paid all her travel expenses.

filing fee Verwaltungsgebühr
There is a filing fee for keeping records of all these particulars.

holding Beteiligung
We have a 25 per cent holding in the company.

Unit 10

home appliance Haushaltsgerät
You may want to buy a washing machine, dish washer or some other home appliance.

home improvement loan Ausbaudarlehen
You get a home improvement loan of your bank to achieve a better standard of your house or flat.

home secured loan Darlehen mit dinglicher Sicherung
You can use your all-purpose home secured loan for any reason you choose.

loan approval Kreditzusage
A loan approval is the permission of a bank to grant an amount of money to a customer.

lump sum Pauschalsumme
You receive a lump sum for a specific purpose and pay off interest and principal over the life of the loan.

penalty Nachteil
Is there a penalty if I pay back the amount I owe all at once?

prepayment vorzeitige Rückzahlung
You can pay your outstanding balance at any time without incurring a prepayment penalty.

prevailing vorherrschend
On variable interest rate loans, the rate moves in line with prevailing market rates.

receivables Forderungen
Interest and dividends receivable amount to 25000 pounds.

revenue account Gewinn- und Verlust-Rechnung
There was a high trading surplus in our last revenue account.

revolving credit erneuerbarer Kredit
Home equity loans can also be a revolving line of credit, available for ten years or more.

shop around den Markt erkunden
Whatever your financial needs, it pays to shop around.

surplus Überschuß
Last year we had a trading surplus of 60 million dollars.

tailor to zuschneiden auf
Loan programs can be tailored to an individual's special situation.

tangible assets materielles Anlagevermögen
About ten per cent of our tangible assets are leased.

title Rechtsanspruch
Title insurance is part of the closing costs for a home equity loan.

turnover Umsatz
Our shop has a turnover of one million a month.

upfront cost Barauslagen
The application fee is often the only upfront cost you must pay at the closing of a loan.

Unit 11

abandon verlassen
The cash stopped because of fears that America would abandon the gold standard.

acquire erwerben
There is no special risk if you acquire fixed-interest securities.

annual general meeting Hauptversammlung
The owners of a PLC can take part in the annual general meeting.

arrears Rückstände
I have fallen into arrears with my rent.

assets Vermögenswerte
There is no risk of losing your money because it is backed by the assets of the company.

bargain-priced günstig bewertet
In the eyes of their investors, American equities look bargain-priced.

bear market Baissemarkt
The bear markets of the late 19th century all sprang form interruptions in the flow of foreign money.

blue chip stocks Standardwerte
Blue chip stocks are common shares of well established companies with a long record of good earnings.

board lot Schluß
The price for the last board lot traded was $27.00.

bonds Schuldverschreibungen
Bonds are issued by various institutions, e.g. the Government or private corporations.

brokerage Maklergebühr
Buyers of shares have to pay brokerage for the service of the market maker.

bull market Haussemarkt
Prices of shares rise in a bull market.

callable shares Aktien mit Rückrufrecht
The issuing company reserves the right to redeem callable shares for cancellation.

closing price Schlußkurs
The price paid for the last board lot was up 25 cents from the closing price in the previous session.

commodity Güter
Prices are fixed at the commodity market in a similar way like at the stock exchange.

common shares Stammaktien
Common shares are issued by a company and represent part ownership in that company.

conversion Umwandlung
Does a conversion really suit your financial needs?

convert umtauschen
Some companies issue bonds that can be converted into stocks after a certain period.

convertible shares Aktien mit Umtauschrecht
Convertible shares may be converted into some other class of stock at a pre-determined price.

coupon Zinsschein
Each type of securities consists of a certificate and the coupon.

cumulative dividend kumulative Dividende
Cumulative dividend must be paid before common dividends are paid.

devalue abwerten
The cash stopped because of fears that America would devalue the dollar.

dividend record Dividendenaufstellung
The price of a stock depends on the earnings, the dividend record and the outlook of a company.

equities Aktien
Equities are common and preferred shares which represent ownership to a company.

exceed übersteigen
If the offers to sell exceed the orders to buy, prices will fall.

face value Nominalwert
The face value of a share is usually much lower than the real value.

fixed-interest securities festverzinsliche Wertpapiere
I would recommend to buy fixed-interest securities instead of shares.

floating rate shares Aktien mit variablem Zins
Floating rate shares pay fluctuating dividend amounts.

futures Termingeschäfte
Futures are contracts to buy or sell specific quantities of a commodity with delivery later.

growth stocks Wachstumspapiere
Growth stocks have excellent prospects for an increase of their real value.

investment certificates Investmentzertifikate
Investment certificates represent equal shares in the portfolio of mutual funds.

investment trust Investmentanteil
Is it more profitable to buy investment trusts as an alternative to shares and bonds?

issue Emission
If there are more orders to buy a given issue than offers to sell, prices will rise.

link Verbindung
Investors in government bonds take for granted the link between the yields on these assets and the ups and downs of currencies.

listed stock börsennotierte Aktien
A stock of a company that is traded on a stock exchange is called listed stock.

overvaluation Überbewertung
One oddity of the global equity market is the overvaluation of Wall Street.

participating shares Aktien mit Gewinnbeteiligung
The holders of participating shares have certain rights to the earnings of a company over their specified dividend rate.

participation Beteiligung
As a shareholder you have the privilege of participation in the company's annual general meeting.

penny stocks Billigaktien
Penny stocks are low-priced, often speculative issues, selling at less than $1.00 a share.

performance Leistung
The amount of the dividend depends on the performance of the company.

portfolio Wertpapierdepot
There is a price risk in the securities' business especially if one's portfolio consists mainly of shares.

preferred shares Vorzugsaktien
Dividends for preferred shares must be paid before any dividends are paid to common shareholders.

prematurely vorzeitig
Depending on the level of interest rates during the term, the company can repay the money prematurely.

price-to-earnings ratio Preis-Gewinn-Verhältnis
A representative basket of American shares would need a price-to-earings ratio of around 11.

prospects Aussichten
The price of a stock reflects investors' opinion of the prospects of that company's shares.

raise money Geld aufbringen
Partnerships cannot raise money at the stock exchange.

redeem einlösen
Stocks are redeemed at a predetermined date.

redeemable shares Aktien mit Rückrufrecht
With redeemable shares the company reserves the right to call them back for cancellation.

retractable shares Aktien mit Rückgaberecht
The holder of retractable shares may hand them in to the company on a specific date at a fixed price.

returns Erträge
The main interest of most shareholders is the price of shares and the returns they can earn.

stock corporation Aktiengesellschaft
A stock corporation produces profits and shareholders are entitled to a dividend.

stock exchange Börse
The prices of shares are fixed at the stock exchange.

trading session Börsenzeit
The highest price paid for the stock during this trading session was $16.00.

unlisted stock Freiverkehrsaktien
An unlisted stock is traded on the over-the-counter market and not at the stock exchange.

utilise nutzen
The mixed portfolio funds try to utilise the benefits of bonds and stocks alike.

variable preferred shares Vorzugsaktien mit variablem Zins
Variable preferred shares pay dividend amounts that fluctuate to reflect changes in interest rates.

voting shares Stimmrechtsaktien
Owners of voting shares possess the right of taking part in decisions in the annual general meeting of the company.

yield Ertrag
Well-informed bank customers try to get a higher yield for their money.

Unit 11

Unit 12

amalgamate verschmelzen
In 1973 all seven stock exchanges in the British Isles amalgamated to form the London Stock Exchange.

automobile-leasing pools Geldanlage im Automobilleasing
Investment in automobile-leasing pools is one of the innovations of American banks.

bonds with warrants Optionsanleihen
Bonds with warrants belong to the new instruments of today's world capital markets.

commission-cutting Provisionsverfall
Most brokers are forced out of business through commission-cutting.

committed engagiert
A firm of brokers has the option of becoming a committed market maker.

consideration ausmachender Betrag
After having fixed the price consideration and brokerage are stipulated in the contract note.

convertible bonds Wandelschuldverschreibungen
In a market with rising share prices convertible bonds are very favourable investments.

dealing systems Abrechnungssysteme
In 1986 the London Stock Exchange introduced new electronic dealing systems.

deep-discount bonds abgezinste Anleihen
There is a higher return on deep-discount bonds than on ordinary bonds with accrued interest.

deregulation Abbau von Vorschriften
On 1 May 1975 deregulation started at the New York Stock Exchange with the abolishment of fixed commissions.

diversify Geschäftsgrundlage erweitern
Many brokers have to seek to diversify, joining a bigger bank grouping.

establishment Gründung
The Industrial Revolution prompted the establishment of more than 30 local share markets in England.

financial options Finanzoptionen
With financial options you can earn a higher yield on your investment.

floor Parkett (Börse)
Before Big Bang a broker went down to the floor asking the jobbers for their prices.

launch auf den Markt bringen
The business firm went to a merchant bank that asked a broker to launch the issue.

liquidity Zahlungsfähigkeit
Liquidity means to have money available that can be immediately used for investment purposes.

market maker Marktmacher (Börse)
To become a market maker means to combine the functions of a broker and a jobber in one firm.

median Mittelwert
The average price of each of the stocks is the median between the bids and offer prices.

merger Fusion
The trouble with the merger route is that you lose your independence.

minimum guaranteed commission Mindestprovision
A system of jobbers and brokers needs minimum guaranteed commissions.

public shares Volksaktien
The British government offered public shares in the state utility Telecom.

reveal offenbaren
The broker asked for the selling and buying price without revealing which interested him particularly.

scramble Kampf
They are forced out of business in a scramble for business through price cutting.

securitized mortgage Briefgrundschuld
A securitized mortgage is easy to transfer to a new lender of money.

sole trader Einzelunternehmer
The jobber is a sole trader and fixes the price at the stock exchange.

solely ausschließlich
The broker acted solely in the interests of the client.

state utility Staatsbetrieb
The British government offered public shares in the state utility British Telecom in New York as well as in London.

stock exchange turnover Börsenumsatzsteuer
When buying shares the investor has to pay stock exchange turnover tax.

take-over Übernahme
A corporation wanting to buy shares in a potential take-over candidate would normally go first to a merchant bank.

underwriting Emissionsübernahme
In Britain banks are restricted from underwriting shares on the market.

accuracy Genauigkeit
No one can forecast future market trends with complete accuracy.

administration Verwaltung
A unit trust investor avoids the inevitable administration which direct share ownership involves.

administrative costs Verwaltungskosten
In terms of administrative costs an investment fund is more economical than direct investment in shares.

advance ansteigen
Prices began to advance strongly again as foreign investment capital flowed back into the German market.

allotment letter Zuteilungsbescheid
You will be requested to surrender any dividends and allotment letters.

assessment Schätzung
Our optimistic assessment of the stock market prompted us to reduce the utility shares in favour of more price-sensitive issues.

balanced fund gemischter Fonds
There is less risk with a balanced fund because you invest in a mix of stocks and bonds.

bid price Geldkurs
Your holding will be sold on the stock exchange at the current market bid price.

blue chip issues Standardwerte
The broadly traded blue chip issues could register strong price gains.

buoyant schwungvoll
The German share market profited from expectations of positive company reports against the background of a buoyant economy.

contract note Schlußnote
If the value of units allocated will be equal to the full offer price of your shares no contract note will be issued.

dealing costs Transaktionskosten
An investment fund is very economical in terms of dealing costs.

ease sich abschwächen
Prices began to rise again as interest rates eased.

economical wirtschaftlich
The investment fund can be more economical than direct investment in terms of administrative and dealing costs.

eligibility Eignung
The manager will advise you on eligibility of your shareholding for inclusion in one of our unit trust portfolios.

global fund Auslandsfonds
In a global fund there are many securities of companies traded on overseas equities markets.

handling fee Bearbeitungsgebühr
The trust company is allowed to deduct a handling fee from the net asset value.

impact Auswirkung
The market suffered a sharp correction under the impact of rising interest rates.

income fund Ertragsfonds
The portfolio of an income fund consists of high-dividend stocks and high-interest bonds.

increment Menge
Shares can be purchased in small increments.

investment manager Anlageberater
The investments of each unit trust are looked after by professional investment managers.

monitor überwachen
Investment managers monitor the fund's holdings and buy and sell shares according to changing market conditions.

mutual fund (US) Investmentfonds
Mutual funds can open the door to the twin benefits of professional money management and portfolio diversification.

offer price Briefkurs
The net proceeds will be allocated to units in the trust at the current offer price less a discount of 2 %.

outnumber zahlenmäßig übertreffen
In sheer quantity, the funds outnumber the companies listed on the Tokyo and New York stock exchanges combined.

portfolio management Depotverwaltung
For individuals with a huge capital to invest finding professional portfolio management is no problem.

portfolio manager Depotverwalter
Our highly experienced team of portfolio managers covers all the major investment markets of the world.

proceeds Erträge
On the next business day the net proceeds of sale will be allocated to units in the trust.

research staff Expertenteam
All the major investment markets are analysed by our research staff.

rights issue Bezugsrechtsausgabe
You will be requested to surrender any allotment letters for rights issues which you may receive after the exchange.

scrip issue Ausgabe von Gratisaktien
You have to surrender any dividends for scrip issues which you may receive after the exchange.

socially conscious fund Ethischer Fonds
Investors in a socially conscious fund want to have their money reinvested according to ethical considerations.

trading volume Handelsvolumen
The uptrend was accompanied by a sharp revival in trading volume.

unit trust (UK) Investmentfonds
If you invest in unit trusts all decisions are taken for you by investment experts.

unit trust investment Investmentanlage
You should be prepared to hold a unit trust investment for a period of at least two years.

valuation Bewertung
No contract note will be issued for your shares but you will be provided with a valuation.

volatile anfällig
Funds that concentrate on a single industry, country or region can be highly volatile.

Unit 14

appreciate — im Wert ansteigen
The pound could either have appreciated or decreased in value.

balance of payments — Zahlungsbilanz
The dollar came under pressure because of a constant balance of payments deficit.

commodity exchange — Warenbörse
Supply and demand determine the prices at the commodity exchange.

convertibility — freie Austauschbarkeit einer Währung
When no restrictions on capital movements exist we speak of full convertibility.

devaluation — Abwertung
Devaluation is a means to enlarge export sales.

exchange control — Devisenkontrolle
Some countries still exercise a more or less strict form of exchange control.

exchange rate — Wechselkurs
Most of the industrialised nations abandoned their fixed exchange rates in the seventies.

fixed exchange rate — fester Wechselkurs
The system of fixed exchange rates came into existence in 1946 following the Bretton Woods agreement.

fixed parities — feste Austauschverhältnisse
The Bretton Woods agreement provided for fixed parities to the dollar, but allowed small variations.

floating exchange rate — flexibler Wechselkurs
Many industrial nations adopted floating exchange rates in the seventies.

forward contract — Termingeschäft
The cost of arranging a forward contract can be considered to be a form of insurance premium.

forward dealing — Terminhandel
Forward dealing on foreign exchange markets is very similar to forward dealing on commodity exchanges.

intervene — eingreifen
In order to keep the rates stable the central bank had to intervene when the lower or upper limit was reached.

revaluation — Aufwertung
The revaluation of the German currency makes exporting German goods more difficult.

Unit 15

air carrier — Luftfrachtführer
The seller fulfills his obligations by delivering the goods to the air carrier at the airport of departure.

air waybill — Luftfrachtbrief
An air waybill is a document accompanying goods transported by air.

bear — tragen
Who will bear the risk of loss or of damage?

carriage — Transport
Who will arrange and pay for the carriage of the goods from one point to another?

certificate of origin — Ursprungszeugnis
You need a certificate of origin to prove that the goods exported were produced in the exporter's country.

civil code — Bürgerliches Gesetzbuch
According to the German civil code the buyer always bears the risk of transport.

civil commotion — öffentliche Tumulte
Special risks such as war and strikes, riots and civil commotion are excluded in the ordinary insurance policy.

clean bill of lading — reines Konnossement
A clean bill of lading must not bear any clause which declares a defective condition of the goods.

compensation — Schadensersatz
The right of compensation from the carrier is limited by means of exceptions and limitations.

congestions — Überfüllung
In countries with peaceful labour conditions the risk of congestions in the ports may be minimal.

consignment note — Güterverkehrsfrachtbrief
The document you need for transporting goods on the road is called consignment note.

consular invoice — Konsulatsfaktura
A consular invoice is proof that the stated price of the exported goods is in conformity with the existing price level.

custody — Verfügungsbereich
The seller fulfills his obligations when he delivers the goods into the custody of the carrier.

customs border — Zollgrenze
The seller's obligations are fulfilled when the goods have arrived at the frontier — but before the customs border.

delivery order — Konnossementsanteilschein
A delivery order is a document authorizing a warehouse to release the stored goods to the person named in the document.

dock warrant — Orderlagerschein
A dock warrant proves the ownership of goods stored in a warehouse at a dock.

evidence — beweisen
The bill of lading evidences the terms of the contract of carriage.

fortuitous — zufällig
The policy covers in principle all risks of fortuitous loss or damage to insured cargo.

fragile — zerbrechlich
Fragile goods that may be particularly liable to damage require more intensive insurance cover.

general average — große Havarie
Sometimes there are costs for salvage or expenses in ports of rescue, so-called general average expenditure.

incur — sich zuziehen
There are costs which may have been incurred on account of measures to save the ship and cargo from a danger.

Unit 15

insurance certificate Einzelpolice
An insurance certificate proves that the holder is covered by insurance.

insurance policy Generalpolice
An insurance policy states the terms under which insurance cover has been provided by an insurer.

marine insurance Seeversicherung
The seller has to procure marine insurance against the risk of loss of or damage to the goods during the carriage.

mate's receipt Steuermannsquittung
The mate's receipt is for goods shipped on board, signed by the mate and used by the ship's master in signing the bill of lading.

negotiable übertragbar
Negotiable means that the goods will be delivered to the holder of the original of the bill of lading.

notification Benachrichtigung
Notification means the duty of each of the parties in an international contract to inform the business partner.

on board bill of lading Bordkonnossement
A received for shipment form of bill of lading has to be converted into a shipped on board bill of lading.

pending bis zu
The buyer may sell the goods to another buyer pending their arrival at the destination.

premises Anwesen
The seller's responsibility is to make the goods available at his premises.

procure beschaffen
The seller has to procure transport insurance against the risk of loss of or damage to the goods during the carriage.

quay Kai
The seller's obligations are fulfilled when the goods have been placed alongside the ship on the quay.

railroad waybill Eisenbahnfrachtbrief
A list of goods sent by rail is called railroad waybill.

salvage Bergungslohn
Salvage is the money paid for the voluntary service of saving a ship or its goods from danger or loss at sea.

tender anbieten
The buyer has to accept delivery of goods upon shipment when the documents have been tendered to him.

trade terms Lieferungsbedingungen
The main purpose of trade terms is to determine at what points the seller has fulfilled his obligations.

warehouse warrant Lagerschein
A warehouse warrant is a receipt for goods deposited in a warehouse giving all details necessary to identify the goods.

wharfinger Kaimeister
A wharfinger is a person who is in charge of a wharf i.e. a quay or pier with warehouses.

wharfinger's warrant Lagerschein
A wharfinger's warrant is a receipt for goods deposited by a wharfinger and gives all details necessary to identify the goods.

Unit 16

advice Ratschlag
Thank you for your advice in your letter dated from ...

advising bank avisierende Bank
The advising bank informs the exporter that a letter of credit was opened to his favour.

certify bestätigen
We enclose a signed invoice in three copies certifying that the goods are in accordance with the order.

commercial invoice Handelsfaktura
The commercial invoice is enclosed in three copies.

dispatch versenden
An air consignment note evidences that the goods have been dispatched.

draft Tratte
The credit is available by drafts drawn at 90 days' sight.

enclose beifügen
I have enclosed your application form with all the relevant details completed.

in accordance with entsprechend
In accordance with your instructions our agents accepted a draft.

in conformity with in Übereinstimmung mit
The bank examines the documents, and if in conformity with the terms of credit, pays the exporter's draft.

irrevocable unwiderruflich
Please open an irrevocable documentary credit in favour of our customer.

issuing bank krediteröffnende Bank
The issuing bank pays for the imported goods in advance.

letter of credit Akkreditiv
The German bank notifies the exporter that the credit is open by means of a letter of credit.

on behalf of im Auftrag von
An irrevocable L/C had been opened by Lloyds Bank on behalf of one of its customers.

on receipt of bei Erhalt
On receipt of the documents the US bank debits the importer's account with the amount of the credit plus expenses.

release übergeben
The US bank releases documents to the importer.

settle ausgleichen
The German bank settles account with the US bank and sends the documents.

triplicate dreifache Ausfertigung
There is a packing list in triplicate among the required documents.

valid gültig
This credit is valid until the end of this year.

Vocabulary German-English

The numbers give you the unit where the word is used.

Abbau von Vorschriften	deregulation *12*
Abfahrt	departure *7*
abgezinste Anleihen	deep-discount bonds *12*
abhängig von	subject to *8*
abheben	withdraw *2*
abholen	collect *7*
Abkürzung	abbreviation *2*
ablaufen	expire *6*
Abonnement	subscription *4*
Abrechnungssysteme	dealing systems *12*
Abrechnungszeitraum	billing period *8*
Abschlagszahlung	lump sum *10*
Abschlußkosten	closing costs *10*
abschreiben	depreciate *10*
abwerten	devalue, depreciate *11, 14*
Abwertung	devaluation *14*
Akkreditiv	letter of credit *16*
Aktien	equities *11*
Aktien mit Gewinnbeteiligung	participating shares *11*
Aktien mit Rückgaberecht	retractable shares *11*
Aktien mit Rückrufrecht	redeemable shares, callable shares *11*
Aktien mit Umtauschrecht	convertible shares *11*
Aktien mit variablem Zins	floating rate shares *11*
Aktiengesellschaft	stock corporation, public limited company *11*
Aktualisierung der Konten	account updating *5*
anbieten	tender *15*
anfällig	volatile *13*
Anforderungen	requirements *7*
Anlageberater	investment adviser *1*
Anspruch	claim *6*
ansteigen	advance *13*
Antrag, Wunschliste	request form *7*
Antragsformular	application form *2*
Anwesen	premises *15*
Anwesen, Grundbesitz	property *9*
Anzahlung	down payment *10*
Arztkosten	medical expenses *7*
auf dem laufenden bleiben	keep track of *8*
auf den Markt bringen	launch *12*
aufliegend, verfügbar	pre-prepared *7*
aufmerksam	attentive *8*
aufschlagen	gross up *3*
Aufstiegschancen	career opportunities *1*
auftreten	occur *8*
Aufwertung	revaluation *14*
Aufzeichnung	record *8*
Ausbaudarlehen	home improvement loan *10*
ausführen	effect *4*
Ausgabe	issue *5*
Ausgabe von Banknoten	note issue *1*
Ausgabe von Gratisaktien	scrip issue *13*
ausgleichen	settle *16*
Auslandsfonds	global fund *13*
ausleihen	borrow *9*
ausmachender Betrag	consideration *12*
ausschließlich	solely *12*
Aussichten	prospects *11*
Aussteller	drawer *6*
Auswirkung	impact *13*
Automatenkarte	cashpoint card *5*
avisierende Bank	advising bank *16*
Baissemarkt	bear market *11*
Bankdienste in der Schalterhalle	lobby banking *5*
Barauslagen	upfront cost *10*
Barscheck	open cheque *6*
Basissteuer auf Zinserträge	basic rate income tax *3*
Basiszinssatz	base rate *9*
Bausparkasse	building society *5*
beanspruchen	claim *6*
beantragen	apply *6*
Bearbeitungsgebühr	handling fee *13*
Begünstigter	beneficiary *4*
behalten	retain *7*
Behinderung	disablement *7*
bei Erhalt	on receipt of *16*
beifügen	enclose *16*
Beleg	voucher *4*
belegloser Zahlungsverkehr	electronic money transmission *5*
Belegschaft	staff *1*
benachrichtigen	notify *6*
Benachrichtigung	notification *15*
Bequemlichkeit	convenience *8*
beraten	advise *9*
Bergungsgebühr	salvage *15*
Berufsschule	vocational school *1*
beschaffen	procure *15*
Beschäftigung	occupation *2*
Besitz	property *9*
Bestandteil	ingredient *7*
bestätigen	certify *16*
bestimmt für	designed for *4*
Bestimmungsort	destination *7*

Beteiligung	participation, holding *10, 11*
Beurteilung	judgment *8*
Beweis	evidence *4*
beweisen	evidence *15*
Bewertung	valuation *13*
bezahlen	foot *7*
Bezogener	drawee *6*
Bezugsrechtsausgabe	rights issue *13*
Bildschirmauskunft	viewing facility *5*
Bildschirmtext	Prestel *5*
Billigaktien	penny stocks *11*
bis zu	pending *15*
Blankoscheck	blank cheque *6*
Blockunterricht	block release *1*
Bordkonnossement	on board bill of lading *15*
Börse	stock exchange *11*
börsennotierte Aktien	listed stock *11*
Börsenumsatzsteuer	stock exchange turnover *12*
Börsenzeit	trading session *11*
Briefgrundschuld	securitized mortgage *12*
Briefkurs	offer price *13*
Bruttogehalt	gross salary *1*
Bürgerliches Gesetzbuch	civil code *15*
Bürgschaft	surety *9*
Darlehen mit Immobilien-Sicherung	home secured loan *10*
Darlehensbetrag	principal *9*
Darlehenskonto	loan account *3*
Darlehenslaufzeit	lending period, term of a loan *9*
Datenträgeraustausch	exchange of data media *5*
Dauerauftrag	standing order *2*
den Markt erkunden	shop around *10*
Depotkonto	safe custody account *3*
Depotverwalter	portfolio manager *13*
Depotverwaltung	portfolio management *13*
Devisenkontrolle	exchange control *14*
Dispositionskredit	overdraft *2*
Dividendenanteil	dividend stamp *10*
Dividendenaufstellung	dividend record *11*
Dividendenschein	dividend stamp *10*
dreifache Ausfertigung	triplicate *16*
echt	genuine *6*
Ehegatte	spouse *9*
Eigenkapital	equity *10*
Eigentum, Besitz	property *6*
Eignung	eligibility *13*
einbehalten	retain *4, 5*
eingreifen	intervene *14*
Einkommensteuererklärung	return of total income *3*
einlösbar	exchangeable *7*
einlösen	honour, redeem *6, 11*
Einreicher	presenter *6*
Einrichtung	establishment *12*
Einrichtungsgegenstände	fittings *9*
einwandfrei	impeccable *6*
Einzahlungsschein	paying-in slip *2*
Einzelangaben	particulars *3*
Einzelhändler	retailer *6*
Einzelpolice	insurance certificate *15*
Einzelunternehmer	sole trader *12*
Eisenbahnfrachtbrief	railroad waybill *15*
Emission	issue *11*
Emissionsübernahme	underwriting *12*
Empfänger	recipient *6*
empfehlen	recommend *9*
engagiert	committed *12*
entsprechend	in accordance with *16*
Entsprechung	equivalent *6*
erlauben	permit *4*
Erlöse	proceeds *6*
ermächtigen	authorize *6*
erneuerbarer Kredit	revolving credit *10*
ersetzen	refund *7*
erstatten	refund, reimburse *7, 9*
Ertrag	yield *11*
Erträge	proceeds, returns *11, 16*
Ertragsfonds	income fund *13*
Erwartung	anticipation *1*
erwerben	acquire *11*
Ethischer Fonds	socially conscious fund *13*
Expertenteam	research staff *13*
falls	in case of *9*
Familienstand	marital status *9*
Faustpfand	dead pledge *9*
Fehler	fault *6*
feste Austauschverhältnisse	fixed parities *14*
fester Wechselkurs	fixed exchange rate *14*
Festgeldkonto	time deposit account *3*
festverzinsliche Wertpapiere	fixed-interest securities *11*
Filiale	local head office *1*
Finanzamt	Inland Revenue *3*
Finanzierungsgebühr	finance charge *8*
Finanzoptionen	financial options *12*
Finanzservice	cash management *5*
flexibler Wechselkurs	floating exchange rate *14*
Forderungen	receivables *10*
Forderungsabtretung	assignment *9*
Frage	query *5*
frei aushandelbar	negotiable *12*
freie Austauschbarkeit e-r Währung	convertibility *14*
Freiverkehrsaktien	unlisted stock *11*
Fusion	merger *12*

Gebühr	fee *2*
gebührenfrei	toll-free *8*
Geheimzahl	code number *4*
Geld aufbringen	raise money *11*
Geldanlage im Automobilleasing	automobile-leasing pools *12*
Geldautomat	cash dispenser *2*
Geldkurs	bid price *13*
Geldpolitik	monetary policy *1*
gelegentlich	odd *7*
Gemeinschaftskonto	joint account *3*
gemischter Fonds	balanced fund *13*
Genauigkeit	accuracy *13*
Generalpolice	insurance policy *15*
Gesamtschuld	joint liability *9*
Geschäftsgrundlage erweitern	diversify *12*
gesetzliche Kündigungsfrist	legal period of notice *3*
Gewinn- und Verlust-Rechnung	revenue account *10*
Girokonto	current account, cheque account *2, 3*
große Havarie	general average *15*
Grundbesitz	real estate *9*
Grundbuch	land register *9*
Grundgebühr	basic charge *2*
Grundschuld	land charge *9*
Gründung	establishment *12*
gültig	valid *16*
günstig bewertet	bargain-priced *11*
Güter	commodity *11*
Güterverkehrsfrachtbrief	consignment note *15*
Guthaben	credit *2*
haftbar	liable for *6*
Handelsfaktura	commercial invoice *16*
Handelsvolumen	trading volume *13*
Hauptstelle	head office *1*
Hauptversammlung	annual general meeting *11*
Haushaltsgerät	home appliance *10*
Haussemarkt	bull market *11*
hochentwickelt	sophisticated *5*
Homebanking	homebanking *5*
Hypothek	mortgage *9*
im Auftrag von	on behalf of *16*
im Ausland	abroad *7*
im Grunde	basically *8*
im Wert ansteigen	appreciate *14*
im Wert sinken	depreciate *10*
in eine Bank eintreten	join a bank *1*
in Übereinstimmung mit	in conformity with *16*
Indossament	endorsement *6*
Inhaberscheck	bearer cheque *6*

Inventar	fixtures *9*
Investmentanlage	unit trust investment *13*
Investmentanteil	investment trust *11*
Investmentfonds	mutual fund (US), unit trust (UK) *13*
Investmentzertifikate	investment certificates *11*
Jahreszinssatz	annual percentage rate (APR) *10*
Kai	quay *15*
Kaimeister	wharfinger *15*
Kampf	scramble *12*
Kasse	till *5*
kaufen	purchase *4*
Konnossementsanteilschein	delivery order *15*
Konsulatsfaktura	consular invoice *15*
Kontoauszug	bank statement *4*
Kontoauszug	statement *2*
Kontoüberziehung	overdraft *9*
Kontrollabschnitt	counterfoil *4*
Kosten	expenses *10*
Krankengeld	hospital benefit *7*
krediteröffnende Bank	issuing bank *16*
Kreditgenossenschaft	credit cooperative *1*
Kreditkarte	credit card *7*
Kreditprüfung	credit assessment *9*
Kreditrahmen	overdraft facility *2*
Kreditzusage	loan approval *10*
kumulative Dividende	cumulative dividend *11*
Kunde	client *8*
Lagerschein	warehouse warrant, wharfinger's warrant *15*
Lastschrift	direct debit *2*
Lehrzeit	apprenticeship *1*
Leihgebühr	rental *8*
Leistung	performance *11*
Lieferant	supplier *9*
liefern	supply *4*
Lieferungsbedingungen	trade terms *15*
Lohnsteuer	pay-as-you-earn (PAYE) *9*
Luftfrachtbrief	air waybill *15*
Luftfrachtführer	air carrier *15*
Maklergebühr	brokerage *11*
Marktmacher (Börse)	market maker *12*
materielles Anlagevermögen	tangible assets *10*
Mehrwertsteuer	value added tax (VAT) *4*
Menge	increment *13*
Mindestprovision	minimum guaranteed commission *12*
Mithaftung	joint liability *9*
Mittel, Potential	resource *8*

Mittelwert	median *12*
Muster	specimen *4*
nachschlagen	look up *9*
Nachteil	penalty *10*
Nachweis	evidence *9*
Niederlassung	establishment *8*
Nominalwert	face value *11*
Notfall	emergency *8*
nutzen	utilise *11*
Nutzen ziehen aus	benefit from *6*
offenbaren	reveal *12*
öffentlich-rechtliches Kreditinstitut	public-law credit institution *1*
öffentlich-rechtliche Sparkasse	trustee savings bank *1*
öffentliche Tumulte	civil commotion *15*
Optionsanleihen	bonds with warrants *12*
Orderlagerschein	dock warrant *15*
Orderscheck	order cheque *6*
Pächter	tenant *9*
Parkett (Börse)	floor *12*
passen	match *9*
passend	appropriate *8*
Pauschalsumme	lump sum *10*
pendeln	commute *1*
Persönliche Kennummer	personal identification number (PIN) *5*
Persönlicher Besitz	Personal property *7*
Persönlicher Kredit	personal loan *9*
Pfand	pledge *9*
Pfandbriefbank	securities depository bank *1*
Pfandrecht	lien *9*
platzen (Scheck)	bounce *6*
Prämie	premium *7*
Preis-Gewinn-Verhältnis	price-to-earnings ratio *11*
Preisnachlaß	discount *1*
Provision	commission *9*
Provisionsverfall	commission-cutting *12*
quittiert	receipted *4*
Quittung	receipt *4*
Rate	instalment *8*
Ratenkauf	hire purchase *9*
Ratschlag	advice *16*
Rechnung	bill *5*
Rechtsanspruch	title *10*
rechtzeitige Kündigung	advance notice *3*
reines Konnossement	clean bill of lading *15*
Reisescheck	travellers' cheque *7*
Rentenbeiträge	superannuation *1*
Rückstände	arrears *11*
Rücktrittsgebühren	cancellation charges *7*

sachdienlich	pertinent to *8*
Saldo	balance *2*
Sammelüberweisung	multiple credit *4*
Schadensersatz	compensation *15*
Schadensersatz leisten	reimburse *7*
Schalterhalle	service hall *5*
schätzen	estimate, assess *3, 9*
Schätzgebühr	appraisal fee *10*
Schätzung	assessment *13*
Scheckabteilung	cheque department *1*
Scheckkarte	cheque guarantee card *4*
Schluß	board lot *11*
Schlußnote	contract note *13*
Schlußkurs	closing price *11*
Schuld	debit *2*
schulden	owe *9*
Schulden übernehmen	discharge *3*
Schuldverschreibungen	bonds *11*
Schutzgebühr	appraisal fee *10*
schwungvoll	buoyant *13*
Seeversicherung	marine insurance *15*
Selbstbedienungsbank	automated teller machine (ATM) *5*
sich abschwächen	ease *13*
sich erkundigen	inquire *8*
sich zuziehen	incur *15*
Skonto	cash discount *4*
Sparkonto	deposit account *3*
Staatsbetrieb	state utility *12*
Stadtsparkasse	municipal savings bank *1*
Stammaktien	common shares *11*
Standardwerte	blue chip issues, stocks *11, 13*
ständiger Wohnsitz	permanent residence *9*
Steuermannsquittung	mate's receipt *15*
Steuerstundung	deferred taxation *10*
Stimmrechtsaktien	voting shares *11*
Stückelung	denomination *7*
tatsächlich	actual *3*
teilhaben	participate *8*
Teilhaberkonto	share account *3*
Teilzeitunterricht	day release *1*
Termingeschäft	forward contract *14*
Termingeschäfte	futures *11*
Terminhandel	forward dealing *14*
Tilgung	repayment of principal *9*
Tochtergesellschaft	subsidiary *1*
tragen	bear *15*
Transaktionskosten	dealing costs *13*
Transport	carriage *15*
Tratte	draft *16*
Trinkgeld geben	tip *7*
TÜV	MOT *1*
Überbewertung	overvaluation *11*
Überfüllung	congestions *15*
übergeben	release *16*

Übernahme take-over *12*
Überschuß surplus *10*
übersteigen exceed *11*
übertragbar negotiable *15*
überwachen monitor *13*
überweisen remit, transfer *2*
Überweisung transfer, remittance *4, 9*
überziehen overdraw *2*
umfassend comprehensive *7*
Umsatz turnover *10*
umtauschen convert *11*
Umwandlung conversion *11*
ungefähr approximately *6*
Unterhalt maintenance *1*
unterhaltsberechtigte Kinder dependent children *9*
Unterkunft accommodation *1*
Unternehmenssektor corporate sector *1*
unterschreiben sign *2*
Unterschriftsprobe specimen signature *2*
Unterstützung back-up *7*
unwiderruflich irrevocable *16*
Ursprungszeugnis certificate of origin *15*

Verabredung appointment *9*
Verantwortung responsibility *4*
Verbindlichkeiten liabilities *9*
Verbindung connection, link *2, 11*
vereinbarte Kündigungsfrist agreed period of notice *3*
verfügbar available *6*
Verfügbarkeit availability *8*
verfügen über draw upon *8*
Verfügung disposal *8*
Verfügungsbereich custody *15*
verhandeln negotiate *6*
Verkaufsbeleg sales voucher *8*
Verkaufspersonal sales staff *9*
Verlangen request *4*
verlassen abandon *11*
Verleih rental *8*
Vermögen asset *10*
Vermögenswerte assets *11*
verpfänden pledge *9*
Verpflichtung liability *7*
Verrechnungsscheck crossed cheque *6*
verschmelzen amalgamate *12*
versenden dispatch *16*
Versicherung insurance *7*
Versicherungsschutz coverage, cover *7, 9*
Versicherungsschutz gewähren cover *7*
versorgen mit provide *4*
verstaatlichen nationalize *1*
Verwaltung administration *13*
Verwaltungsgebühr filing fee *10*
Verwaltungskosten administrative costs *13*
Verwaltungszentrale registered office *1*
verwandt mit related to *1*
Visum visa *7*
Volksaktien public shares *12*
Vollmacht power of attorney *2*
vorher bereitgestellt pre-prepared *7*
vorherrschend prevailing *10*
Vorschußzins advance interest *3*
Vorschuß advance *9*
vorzeitig prematurely *11*
vorzeitige Rückzahlung prepayment *10*
Vorzugsaktien preferred shares *11*
Vorzugsaktien mit variablem Zins variable preferred shares *11*

Wachstumspapiere growth stocks *11*
Wahlrecht option *9*
Währung currency *6*
Wandelschuldverschreibungen convertible bonds *12*
Warenbörse commodity exchange *14*
Wechseldiskontierung bill discounting *9*
Wechselkurs exchange rate *14*
wegen due to *5*
weitergeben negotiate *6*
Wertpapierdepot portfolio *11*
wettbewerbsfähig competitive *9*
widerrufen countermand *6*
Widerwillen reluctance *5*
wirtschaftlich economical *13*

zahlenmäßig übertreffen outnumber *13*
Zahlungsbilanz balance of payments *14*
Zahlungsempfänger payee *4*
Zahlungsfähigkeit liquidity *12*
Zahlungsverzug default on payment *9*
zerbrechlich fragile *15*
Zins interest *2*
Zinsertrag interest received *3*
Zinsschein coupon *11*
Zollgrenze customs border *15*
zufällig fortuitous *15*
Zugang access *5*
zurückfordern reclaim *3*
zurückkaufen redeem *9*
zurückverfolgen trace back *6*
Zusammenbau, Montage assembly *9*
zusammenfassen consolidate *10*
zusätzliche Sicherheit collateral *10*
Zusatzprovision excess commission *7*
zuschneiden auf tailor to *10*
Zuteilungsbescheid allotment letter *13*
Zweck purpose *4*
Zweigstelle branch *1*
Zweigstellennetz branch network *5*

English Word List

The numbers give you the unit where the word is used.

abandon *11*
abbreviation *2*
abroad *7*
access *5*
accommodation *1*
account updating *5*
accuracy *13*
acquire *11*
actual *3*
administration *13*
administrative costs *13*
advance *9*
advance *13*
advance interest *3*
advance notice *3*
advice *16*
advise *6*
advising bank *16*
agreed period of notice *3*
air carrier *15*
air waybill *15*
allotment letter *13*
amalgamate *12*
annual general meeting *11*
annual percentage rate (APR) *10*
anticipation *1*
application form *2*
apply *6*
appointment *9*
appraisal fee *10*
appreciate *14*
apprenticeship *1*
appropriate *8*
approximately *6*
arrears *11*
assembly *9*
assess *3*
assessment *13*
asset *10*
assets *11*
assignment *9*
attentive *8*
authorize *6*
automated teller machine (ATM) *5*
automobile-leasing pools *12*
availability *8*
available *6*
back-up *7*
balance *2*
balance of payments *14*
balanced fund *13*
bank statement *4*
bargain-priced *11*
base rate *9*
basic charge *2*
basic rate income tax *3*
basically *8*
bear *15*
bear market *11*
bearer cheque *6*
beneficiary *4*
benefit from *6*
bid price *13*
bill *5*
bill discounting *9*
billing period *8*
blank cheque *6*
block release *1*
blue chip issues *13*
blue chip stocks *11*
board lot *11*
bonds *11*
bonds with warrants *12*
borrow *9*
bounce *6*
branch *1*
branch network *5*
brokerage *11*
building society *5*
bull market *11*
buoyant *13*
callable shares *11*
cancellation charges *7*
career opportunities *1*
carriage *15*
cash discount *4*
cash dispenser *2*
cash management *5*
cashpoint card *5*
certificate of origin *15*
certify *16*
cheque account *3*
cheque department *1*
cheque guarantee card *4*
civil code *15*
civil commotion *15*
claim *6*
clean bill of lading *15*
client *8*
closing costs *10*
closing price *11*
code number *4*
collateral *10*
collect *7*
commercial invoice *16*
commission *9*
commission-cutting *12*
committed *12*
commodity *11*
commodity exchange *14*
common shares *11*
commute *1*
compensation *15*
competitive *9*
comprehensive *7*
congestions *15*
connection *2*
consideration *12*
consignment note *15*
consolidate *10*
consular invoice *15*
contract note *13*
convenience *8*
conversion *11*
convert *11*
convertibility *14*
convertible bonds *12*
convertible shares *11*
corporate sector *1*
counterfoil *4*
countermand *6*
coupon *11*
cover *7*
cover *9*
coverage *7*
credit *2*
credit assessment *9*
credit card *7*
credit cooperative *1*
crossed cheque *6*
cumulative dividend *11*
currency *6*
current account (C/A) *2*
custody *15*
customs border *15*
day release *1*
dead pledge *9*
dealing costs *13*
dealing systems *12*
debit *2*
deep-discount bonds *12*
default on payment *9*
deferred taxation *10*
delivery order *15*
denomination *7*
departure *7*
dependent children *9*
deposit account *3*
depreciate *10*
deregulation *12*
designed for *4*
destination *7*
devaluation *14*
devalue *11*
direct debit *2*
disablement *7*
discharge *3*
discount *1*
dispatch *16*
disposal *8*
diversify *12*
dividend record *11*
dividend stamp *10*
dock warrant *15*
down payment *10*
draft *16*
draw upon *8*
drawee *6*
drawer *6*
due to *5*
ease *13*
economical *13*
effect *4*
electronic money transmission *5*
eligibility *13*
emergency *8*

List of Abbreviations

APR	annual percentage rate Jahreszinssatz	Unit 10
ATM	Automated Teller Machine Selbstbedienungsbank	Unit 5
B/E	Bill of Exchange Wechsel	Unit 6
B/L	Bill of Lading Konnossement	Unit 15
BACS	Bankers Automated Clearing Services Elektronischer Überweisungsverkehr	Unit 5
BACSTEL	BACS via a telephone Elektronischer Überweisungs-verkehr per Telefon	Unit 5
C/A	Current Account Girokonto	Unit 3
CFR	Cost and Freight Kosten und Fracht (C&F)	Unit 15
CHAPS	Clearing House Automated Payments System Automatisches Clearing im Zahlungsverkehr	Unit 5
CIF	Cost, Insurance and Freight Kosten, Versicherung, Fracht	Unit 15
CIP	Freight Carriage and Insurance Paid to Frachtfrei versichert	Unit 15
DAF	Delivered at Frontier Geliefert Grenze	Unit 15
DCP	Freight Carriage Paid to Fracht, Porto bezahlt bis	Unit 15
DDP	Delivery Duty Paid Geliefert verzollt	Unit 15
dept	department Abteilung	Unit 1
DEQ	Delivery Ex Quay Geliefert ab Kai (verzollt)	Unit 15
EFTPOS	Electronic Funds Transfer at the Point of Sale Elektronischer Zahlungsverkehr über Kassenterminals	Unit 5
EXQ	Ex Quay Ab Kai	Unit 15
EXS	Ex Ship Ab Schiff	Unit 15
EXW	Ex Works Ab Werk	Unit 15
FAS	Free Alongside Ship Frei Längsseite Seeschiff	Unit 15
FOB	Free on Board Frei an Bord	Unit 15
FOR	Free on Rail Frei Waggon	Unit 15
FCA	Free Carrier Frei Frachtführer	Unit 15
IMO	International Money Order Internationale Zahlungsanweisung	Unit 4
L/C	Letter of Credit Akkreditiv	Unit 16
Ltd	Limited GmbH	Unit 1
MOT	Ministry of Transport TÜV – Technischer Überwachungs-verein	Unit 1
OTC	Over-the-counter market Freiverkehrsmarkt	Unit 11
pa	per annum pro Jahr	Unit 2
PAYE	pay-as-you-earn Lohnsteuer	Unit 9
PIN	Personal Identification Number Persönliche Kennummer	Unit 5
PLC	Public Limited Company Aktiengesellschaft	Unit 1
VAT	value-added tax Mehrwertsteuer	Unit 4